Together

Together

Making Your Marriage Better

Jack H. Grossman, Ph.D.

Contemporary Books, Inc.
Chicago

Library of Congress Cataloging in Publication Data

Grossman, Jack H.
    Together, making your marriage better.

    1. Marriage.   2. Interpersonal relations.
3. Interpersonal communication.   I. Title.
HQ734.G835   1982   646.7'8   82-45438
ISBN 0-8092-5646-0

Published by Contemporary Books, Inc.
180 North Michigan Avenue, Chicago, Illinois 60601
Manufactured in the United States of America
Library of Congress Catalog Card Number: 82-45438
International Standard Book Number: 0-8092-5646-0

Published simultaneously in Canada by
Beaverbooks, Ltd.
150 Lesmill Road
Don Mills, Ontario M3B 2T5
Canada

To Joan
My partner, best friend, wife, and
mother of our children

Contents

Together

Introduction

BECAUSE none of us is flawless, no marriage can possibly be perfect. Those who seek perfection in their marriage, and do not allow themselves to enjoy a relationship that falls short of this unrealistic expectation, are doomed to a search that can only lead to frustration and unhappiness. No book, including this one, can help such individuals.

If your desires are realistic, however, and you would be satisfied with a marriage whose quality is somewhere on the positive end of a range that goes from perfection to misery, this book is for you. Regardless of where you fit within this broad range, there is always room for improvement.

If your motives are similar to those of most people, you married (or remarried) and want to remain married because you perceive this type of relationship to be more meaningful than any others you may have considered. You believe that marriage offers certain benefits and rewards that might not otherwise be available to you.

The extent to which you are experiencing whatever emotional, physical and intellectual pleasures you anticipated, hoped for, or grew to want is a good measure of how successful your marriage is.

Couples who have highly successful marriages are able and willing to adapt to each other's growing and changing needs and wants. They are willing to discuss these changes and bend somewhat to accommodate one another. Each cares enough about the other to make every effort to understand and respond to his or her partner's desires. Both are willing to do all that and more because the emotional bond that draws them together is strong, and they want to keep it that way.

Those couples who don't have a good marriage behave differently. They take each other for granted, are inconsiderate of their mates, and basically act *as if* they were independent rather than interdependent. In short, they want the benefits of marriage without making the appropriate investments; they will take what they can from their mates without giving much in return.

No relationship in which one person does most of the giving and the other the taking can last very long. If it does, it certainly can't be a satisfying relationship for either person. The only way a couple can have the pleasure they hoped for when they married is for both to give of themselves to the other. However, knowing what to give requires both of you to be sensitive to each other's needs and desires. By listening carefully with your eyes and your ears, and by taking note of your partner's actions and reactions, you will have all the clues you need for giving your fair share.

If your partner is not all that sensitive, you have an obligation to yourself and your mate to make your needs and wants known to him or her. In so doing you will increase your chances of receiving your fair share. This approach certainly is more reasonable than playing guessing games. The direct approach to getting what you want will not be new to either of you. Don't you know what is required of you in your job, or what you need to do to advance in your career? In school, didn't you know what you had to do to attain the grades you wanted? While the concept I'm suggesting is no different, the specific methods for obtaining and conveying this vital information *is* different and will be discussed in this book.

The notion that a single marriage agreement or philosophy is right for everybody is a myth. Every couple has to discover for themselves what works and doesn't work for *them*. At the same time, there are some basic principles that, when practiced, can aid you in finding out what you need from each other, communicating your needs effectively, and discussing your individual or mutual problems or concerns. These principles, which are discussed in Parts I and II, can serve as useful guides in *any* interdependent relationship. That is, you can apply these principles at work, with your friends, or with other relatives you care about. However, the exercises you will be asked to do in Part III are designed specifically to help you and your spouse determine the kind of marital relationship both of you want it to be. While it may be different from what your neighbors, relatives, or friends want in a marriage, it will be right for you. That is all that really matters, isn't it? Once you determine what you want from each other, I will show you how to fulfill these desires.

The road to a mutually rewarding partnership is not easy. If both of you want to make it work, however, this book can help you. Just recognize that this book is not a magical pill that will eliminate all problems. Nor is it a panacea for couples who are emotionally divorced from each other, i.e., when the spark in the relationship is gone. It is, however, for couples who care enough about each other to take the steps necessary to rekindle the fire and revitalize the magnetic force that first drew them together. It is also useful for couples who are about to be married. In this book, engaged couples will find guidelines for *preventing* their relationships from deteriorating in the first place.

Together: Making Your Marriage Better affirms my belief that a lasting and healthy marital relationship cannot be based strictly on the physical or emotional forces that attract two people to each other. While I would not undermine their importance, the major cause of dull relationships, major discords, extramarital affairs, and divorces is *not* sexual incompatibility. Rather, it is the failure of one or both parties to honor the promises and commitments they made and implied when they exchanged their marriage vows.

I have known sexually compatible couples who did not have good marriages. For these people sex not only did not have the magical powers that "experts" impute to it, but the quality and frequency of their sexual contacts diminished when their personal relationships deteriorated. My belief that sex is not enough to make a marriage work is constantly supported by couples who have drifted apart and are now having an affair. When I ask, "What is the main attraction of the new person you are seeing?" almost invariably they reply, "I can talk to him (or her)," or "He (or she) cares about me," or "He (or she) pays attention to me." Rarely does anyone say, "He (or she) is better in bed." The obvious conclusion is that for a marriage to endure successfully (assuming that sexual compatibility is not an issue), it has to be nourished with mutual respect, trust, and loving attitudes.

If you are to withstand the pressures and overcome those problems you face as a couple, and if you desire a vibrant, enjoyable, lifelong friendship with your mate, you must know yourself, your partner, and what it takes to help each other become the person you are capable of being. My intention in this book is to help you achieve these objectives, as well as to help you develop the kind of marriage that will please both of you.

One caution before we proceed: This is not a book to be read as you would a novel. Rather, it is like a gourmet cookbook, whose directions must be followed carefully without skipping steps. You can't rush. After all, we're talking about a gourmet marriage, which cannot be achieved with a simple recipe of platitudes and clichés. A marriage of this rare quality requires tender, loving care and attention to important details. It requires two mature adults who have the basic ingredients of a good marriage and are committed to making it work, but who need to learn how to put the ingredients together.

If you qualify, let's begin.

PART I

Learning How to Communicate
Effectively

1

Communication: The Bridge That Connects Two Worlds

You and your spouse come from two different worlds. While you are similar in some respects, you come from different backgrounds, have different personalities and different dispositions. These differences are reflected in your values, self-image, goals, interests, desires, energy levels, and reactions to various people and events.

When you married, you, in effect, merged your two distinct worlds into one. You did it through the process of communication. That process was the bridge that connected your respective worlds and allowed you to learn what you could about each other. You then had a choice as to how you wanted to respond to that information. This bridge continues to be a means of maintaining contact and exchanging information as each of you changes and grows. When that bridge becomes defective or you make the wrong choice, your relationship suffers.

Healthy relationships are distinguished by the quality of their communications. What you communicate, how you communicate, when you communicate (i.e., your timing), and the spirit with which you and your spouse receive each other's messages will affect your marriage. When people complain of having communication problems, one or several of these issues will likely be the cause.

No relationship I know of requires greater communication skills than marriage. When you consider the closeness of this relationship, the wide range of subjects married couples normally talk about, the breadth of emotions that come into play when discussing issues and handling problems that concern both of them, and the personal idiosyncracies with which both partners must learn to live, it's not hard to believe that this is a skill that takes a lifetime to master. Practicing the principles discussed here and in Part II will give you a good start.

READING BETWEEN THE LINES

"You just don't understand me." "Why can't I get through to you?" "Talking to you is like talking to a wall." "You're so damn insensitive."

Such common complaints suggest that the person on the receiving end may, at best, be hearing words only. The *real* message is not getting through.

Most messages people send consist of two elements. The *rational* component of the message, which often represents only a fraction of its total meaning, is generally transmitted by the words we use. But the more significant element of a message is the *emotion* behind the words. These are conveyed by tone of voice, body language, and other nonverbal expressions, as well as the actual words. The words we choose in conveying a message frequently camouflage its meaning.

Consider the statement, "Do we *always* have to do what *you* want?" This question, as it stands, simply requires a "yes" or "no" response. However, judging from the emphasis, this person is upset and really is expressing the feeling that he does not have much of a say in how they spend their time together. Like most of us, this individual does not come right out and say what is upsetting him, but it is implied by the way he asks the question.

Let's look at a few more examples of what people *say* versus what they actually *mean*.

Statement: "Do you *really* think we can afford a vacation *now?*"
Actual Meaning: "I have some doubts about whether we can afford this luxury now. I need to be convinced that taking this vacation will not strap us financially. I'm feeling insecure about our financial situation."

Statement: "I can't remember the last time we went out *alone.*"
Actual Meaning: "We don't seem to be enjoying each other's company since we need others to entertain us. Am I not as much fun or as interesting as I used to be?"

Statement: "I wish you wouldn't spend so much time on the phone."
Actual Meaning: "I feel neglected; I feel I'm not as important to you as others are."

When you detect that a statement or question contains a hidden or even blatant emotional message, it is imperative that you respond to that message *first*. Your response will encourage your spouse to keep talking until he has expressed his feelings. It also tells him that you care about that which is *really* important to him. Later, after the emotions have been vented, you may talk about the rational part of the message. Or, if you like, you may ask questions so you can understand what caused the feelings.

If you realize that a two-part message is like an iceberg, with the words representing only the tip of that iceberg, you will appreciate the importance and magnitude of the emotional segment of a message. Failure to penetrate the surface of the message does not cause the emotional portion to vanish. Rather, these neglected feelings tend to become exaggerated and distorted. When you least expect it, they can erupt in the form of angry accusations.

The fact that all of us say and do things that don't make sense but *feel* right at the time attests to the power of such emotions as joy, anger, sadness, frustration, disgust, fear, excitement, and ecstasy. However, these and other emotions are nonrational; therefore, they cloud our sense of reason. The power of these emotions, combined with their nonrational nature, explains why people who are temporarily not in control of their emotions are not responsive to rational arguments or points of view. An individual's emotional state is far more significant to him than his thoughts and even overshadows his concerns about what is or is not an appropriate response. Consequently, when you ignore those emotions, you are telling that person that you don't care about the feelings he is experiencing at the moment. Wouldn't *you* be upset if someone disregarded something that was so important to you?

Responding to the emotional part of a statement first, and then to its rational content, applies even if your spouse presents a problem to which you are tempted to offer a quick and possibly reasonable solution. Before offering practical help, let her know that you sense her discomfort. Or, if he is joyful about something, let him know that you share his excitement before suggesting that you celebrate the occasion.

The most appropriate response to an emotional message is to acknowledge it. You can do this with such statements as: "I sense that you're bothered by _____"; "I can appreciate your concern about _____"; "Sounds like you're pleased with _____."

Statements of acknowledgment should convey your appreciation for the fact that the person is saying more than the words themselves express. By the way, silence accompanied by a look of concern can also be very effective, as can repeating a portion of a statement. While your specific responses may vary, the attitude you must convey is, "I realize that there is more to what you are telling me than what you're actually saying. If you want to elaborate, the door is open to you."

Here are three examples that illustrate what I mean by appropriate responses; they are followed by responses that *fail* to acknowledge the emotions conveyed.

Statement: "Nobody around here gives a damn about me."
Suggested Response: "Sounds like you're upset about something."
                        ]OR[
    "What gives you that impression?"
Rational Response: "Yes they do."

Statement: "Do you *have* to go to the meeting tonight?"
Suggested Response: "Are you saying that you'd rather I not go?"
                        ]OR[
    Does that upset you?"
Rational Response: "Yes, I do."
                        ]OR[
    "No I don't *have* to go, but I want to."

Statement: "Boy, did I have a rough day today."
Suggested Response: "Oh?"
                        ]OR[
    "Rougher than usual?"
                        ]OR[
    "Do you want to tell me about it?"
Rational Response: "*Every day* is tough for me."
                        ]OR[
    "That's the way it is sometimes."
                        ]OR[
    "You think *you* had a hard day."

As you can see, each of the suggested responses is an implied invitation to talk about the feelings that prompted the statement. While the *ultimate* resolution to the initial statement may indeed be rational, that resolution is easier to accept (even if somewhat painful) when your spouse is allowed to express her feelings first. *Immediate* rational reactions, however, shut the door to further communications. More than likely they would cause the other person to become angry or stew about the feelings that prompted the statement.

Another factor to consider when responding to emotions is that each person's feelings are unique and therefore valid for that person. What excites, angers, or disappoints one person may affect another person differently. That does not make either person wrong or right. Remember, emotions are never right or wrong; they just *are*. For this reason it is inappropriate to judge or criticize a person's feelings; nor is it appropriate to say, "I know how you feel." How can anyone *know* what someone else is feeling? Even if you had a similar experience, the emotions it engendered undoubtedly were different in each case, so you don't really *know* how or what others feel.

Well-meaning people often say to friends, "You shouldn't let it get you down; it could be worse," or "You should be grateful that you are alive," or "You shouldn't cry." On the surface such comments sound reassuring; the fact is, however, that they are not at all helpful. Telling people that they should or shouldn't feel a particular way denies them the right to their unique emotions. It also suggests that there is a standard way of feeling and closes the door to the individuals so they are reluctant to release their emotions fully.

The fruitlessness of judging emotions is illustrated in the following example: Suppose you received a substantially lower raise in pay than you anticipated. You tell your spouse, "I'm really mad that I didn't get a bigger raise." He then replies, "You shouldn't get mad. At least you've got a job, which is more than other people have." Does that reply minimize the anger or hurt that was expressed in the initial statement? Does it help the person cope with her anger or hurt? A more constructive reaction would be, "I guess it must be upsetting not to get what you feel you deserve. What do you plan to do about it?"

Let's consider another example. Your spouse says, "Gee, I'm tired." You reply, "You're *always* tired," or "What have *you* got to be tired about?" As you can see, these judgmental replies not only disregard the emotional content of the statement, but they can also put the person on the defensive or make him angry. A more constructive response, such as "You must have had a rough day," conveys a caring attitude and, as in the previous example, allows the person to elaborate if he so desires.

To summarize, there are three points to remember when responding to emotions or two-part messages that are both rational and emotional in content:

1. Respond first to the emotional part of the message by acknowledging the feeling that is expressed or implied.

2. After the person has *fully* expressed his emotions, respond to the rational part.

3. Do not judge other people's emotions since they are valid for the person experiencing them.

Study the following dialogue so you can see how these principles actually work.

SHE: Even when we're together I feel alone.

HE: Even when we're together? (This acknowledges the emotion by repeating a portion of the statement in the form of a question.)

SHE: Yes.

HE: (Silence) Are you saying that I'm not good company? (This is an attempt to clarify what she meant by her statement.)

SHE: It's just that you're constantly preoccupied with your thoughts or you're usually busy doing something—anything but paying attention to me.

HE: I'm sorry, I didn't realize it. (This gives her another opportunity to vent more of her feelings if she chooses to.)

SHE: Well, that's just the way I feel.

HE: I'll tell you what: From now on, when we're together, I'll make an effort to *really* be with you. OK? (This statement deals with the rational part of her statement.)

Notice that at no point did he give the impression that her feelings were silly, ridiculous, or unreasonable. Furthermore, his suggested remedy came only after her feelings were fully vented.

RECEIVING CRITICISM

Many people do not take criticism well. Typically they respond by justifying, or making excuses for, the behavior being criticized.

Some attack the critic with countercriticisms, and others become either defensive or so angry and upset that they can say nothing at all, *thinking* nasty thoughts that are revealed at a later time, when the critic least expects them. Each of these reactions sets up conditions for a "you're wrong, I'm right" type of dialogue, which is generally destructive.

Consider the following dialogue, which begins with a criticism:

HE: Whenever I get into an argument with your mother you take *her* side. Do you know how that makes me feel?
SHE: But she's my *mother*, and I don't want to hurt her feelings.
HE: What about *my* feelings? Don't they count?
SHE: That's not the point.
HE: Well, what is the point?
SHE: Forget it; you wouldn't understand.
HE: She's obviously more important to you than I am.
SHE: If that's what you want to think, that's OK with me. (She stalks out of the room.)

The combination of conditions—this woman's justification for her action, her failure to discuss his concerns, and her apparent disregard for his feelings—is almost certain to create a cold war and future interpersonal problems. The man, on the other hand, is so intent on making her feel guilty with his comment, "What about *my* feelings? Don't they count?" that he fails to respond appropriately to her statement about not wanting to hurt her mother's feelings.

This discussion could have been more productive had the woman been sensitive to her spouse's feelings without sacrificing her desire to avoid hurting her mother. For example, she could have said, "I don't mean to hurt you, but at the same time I don't want to hurt her either. What do you suggest?" Such a comment would appease him and also engage his help in the solution of her problem. He, on the other hand, could have responded to her comment, "But she's my *mother*...." by saying something like this: "Yes, I know you don't want to hurt your mother's feelings.

But I also know you don't want to hurt mine. Can we work out some way you can handle it so neither of us is hurt?" That type of reaction would not only demonstrate a sensitivity for the woman's reluctance to hurt her mother; it also would convey the feeling that he wants to help her with this dilemma.

One of the more common nonproductive responses to criticism is countercriticism. These reactions are based on the notion that the best defense is an offense. However, when the person you are offending is your spouse such tactics can only prove disastrous. They result in a win-lose situation at best, a lose-lose situation at worst. Consider, for example, these two reactions:

"You say I've been moody lately. Well, let me tell you that *you* haven't been all that friendly either."

"You have some nerve telling me that I spend too much money on my hobbies. Do you realize how much money *you* spend on dumb things?"

No useful purpose is served by countercriticism. All it does is create ill feelings and barriers to good communication.

What, then, is a more appropriate way of reacting to criticism? That depends on whether you agree or disagree with the critic. In either case, you must realize that *all criticism is valid from the critic's perspective.* What others see, feel, and believe is correct from *their* vantage point. Admittedly, their perceptions or interpretations may be distorted or different from yours, but that is the way they see things. For this reason, if you *initially* respond to the critic by implying or actually telling him he is wrong, you will most certainly cause him to defend his position and pave the way for a needless offensive-defensive argument. The fact is that no one likes to be accused of perceptual distortions or of misrepresentations.

In dealing with criticism you *first* should acknowledge that person's perception, whether or not you agree. That acknowledgment allows the person to elaborate so you can learn more about the reasons for the criticism. Then, if you disagree, either present your views and any evidence you have that supports your views or ask for clarification. Consider the following examples of appropriate responses to criticisms that one might *disagree* with:

Criticism: "You're never around when I need you."
Suggested Responses: "I'm not?"

]OR[

"I didn't realize that; I thought I was."

Criticism: "You spend more time on the phone than you do with me."
Suggested Response: "I wasn't aware of that; I thought we spent a lot of time together."

]OR[

"I do?"

Criticism: "No matter what I do for you, it's never enough."
Suggested Response: "What have I said or done to give you that impression?"

]OR[

"Gee, I'm so sorry you feel that way, but that's just not true; I appreciate everything you do."

Notice that each of the suggested responses leaves the door open for a meaningful dialogue. Here are several others you might consider:

- "I'm sure that's the way it looks to you, but may I tell you how I see it?"
- "I'm sorry you feel I ignored you, since that was not my intent. It's just that I've been preoccupied with a number of problems."
- "I don't mean to bug you about it, but it bothers me when you do that. How would *you* suggest that I let you know of my desire?"

The exact words you use are not as important as the message you want to convey. The message is that you respect the criticism and wish to know the reason for it. However, because your perspective on the behavior being criticized is also important, you want to express it. Your objective in the ensuing dialogue should be to reach a mutual understanding. It obviously takes a mature person to respect someone's criticism, but think of the benefits you derive from it.

There will, of course, be times when you *agree* with the criticism. Under those conditions the only sensible response is to concur with the perception, which is another way of acknowledging it, and then offer an explanation for your behavior or a plan for correcting whatever was criticized. Comments such as, "OK, you've got a good point," or "You're right," followed by your explanations, by a statement about the corrective steps you intend to take, or by a request for help to correct the criticized behavior should do it.

To demonstrate how this works in practice, study the following three responses by someone who agrees with the criticism.

Criticism: "When I ask you what's new at work you always say, 'Nothing.' But, if someone calls from the office, you have all kinds of things to talk about."

Response: "That's right. But the reason I say that nothing is new is that when I come home from work I want to relax. The last thing I want to do is rehash what went on there. When someone calls me from work I don't have much of a choice."

Criticism: "Whenever we go to a party I don't see you from the time we get there to the time we leave."

Response: "I'm sorry, but I didn't realize it bothered you. Would you prefer that I visit with the same people you do, even though they may not interest me?"

Criticism: "Lately, when I've felt romantically inclined and tried to tell you, you just haven't responded."

Response: "The reason I wasn't responsive is that I haven't been feeling very well. I guess I should have told you, but I didn't want to upset you."

As in the previous examples, these responses leave the door open to a dialogue that can prove beneficial to both parties. In formulating your response to a criticism, remember that criticisms and emotions are similar and, therefore, responses are governed by the same principles.

Let's consider two more examples of appropriate responses to criticisms you agree with.

Criticism: "You constantly find fault with my family. Can't you ever say anything good about them?"
Suggested Response: "I suppose I have been critical of them, but that's because I feel they don't like me."

Criticism: "I'm tired of hearing you complain about our financial situation."
Suggested Response: "You're right; I have been complaining a lot. So why don't we talk about what we can do to correct it?"

Admittedly, responding to criticism in this way is difficult. The most natural reaction is to become upset, angry, and defensive or offensive. From past experience you know that your natural reactions do not necessarily serve your best interests. In fact, they can, and often do, work against you. It might be easier to put into practice the principles offered here if you realize that criticism is nothing more than a reaction to a problem or hurt the critic is experiencing. Responding critically to the person's problem merely compounds it. If you acknowledge its existence and then express whatever concerns or explanations you have to offer, however, you will contribute to a win-win resolution.

OFFERING CRITICISM

As with receiving criticism, there are appropriate and inappropriate ways of offering it. When you are critical of someone, it is because something that person did, said, did not do, or did not say bothered you. In expressing anger toward someone it is not uncommon to generalize, revert to name calling, and level accusatory remarks toward the *total* person. Phrases such as *"You are* inconsiderate," *"You are* irresponsible," "You *never"* do this or "You *always"* do that are generally inaccurate and destructive and engender defensive reactions. While individual *actions* may be irresponsible or inconsiderate, people rarely exhibit those characteristics in every facet of their life. It is, therefore, understandable to react adversely to such personal attacks. Similarly, "You *always"* or "You *never"* types of statements dilute the message you want to convey, since one can usually find exceptions to such generalizations.

One reason people generalize and label others, particularly when they are angry, is because they feel the criticism will make a greater impression. Another reason is that it simply is easier to lash out at someone than to think about whether or not the words are truthful, make sense, and have value in altering the other person's behavior. While it is unquestionably easier to lash out at those we care about, without giving any thought to what we say, the impression we make tends to alienate them rather than get their attention.

A contructive alternative to castigating the total person, generalizing, or labeling is to *criticize specific acts*, i.e., what a person did or did not say or do that disturbed you. Remember, you can love the sinner and hate the sin, so criticize the sin, not the sinner.

To illustrate how this approach to offering criticism works, let's examine some statements that violate the principle and some constructive alternatives to the same complaints.

Criticism: "You are inconsiderate." (Is the person really inconsiderate or did he *do* something that was inconsiderate?)
Constructive Alternative: "I wish you had let me know you'd be this late for our appointment."

Criticism: "You are always putting me down." (Always? Whenever they're together?)
Constructive Alternative: "I was embarrassed and felt foolish when you said _____ at the party."

Criticism: "I don't like your attitude." (What did he say or do that suggests a bad attitude?)

Constructive Alternative: "The last few times I asked you to come with me to see my folks I had the feeling that I was imposing on you."

Criticism: "You never help around the house." (Never?)

Constructive Alternative: "Since we both work, I think we *both* should have certain responsibilities with regard to taking care of the house."

As you can see, the constructive alternatives are more precise and direct, are not particularly disparaging of the other person, and focus on specific behaviors that can be altered.

This leads to another principle to remember when offering criticism: Don't harp on mistakes, misdemeanors, or problems that cannot be solved. What's done is done. While you can make *reference* to the past as a guide to future actions, to focus on it is of no value. Presumably the person feels bad enough already. Adding salt to the wound does not solve problems; it only exacerbates them. That's why I cringe when I hear someone say, "I told you so," to a person who is upset about something he did that didn't work out well.

Since yesterday is history, all we can do is learn from mistakes we made or revel in the joy of our accomplishments. To dwell on a person's past errors or oversights is counterproductive. Sound advice as this is, the world is loaded with people who seem to achieve pleasure from hitting others over the head with reminders of their past errors. If you are angry or upset over a particular action or reaction, you have every right to make your displeasure known. But to keep bringing it up is fruitless, since the person can change only *future* actions, not what has already occurred. Statements such as "You should have ____," or "If you hadn't ____," should be replaced with "Next time, please _____."

The following two sets of contrasting dialogues illustrate the differences between constructive and destructive approaches to the same problems.

Dialogue 1—Destructive

SHE: God, I hate going to work.

HE: For the past three months you've done nothing but complain about your job. That's all you've done.

SHE: I didn't realize I sounded that bad. I'll stop complaining.

HE: Do you know what it's like hearing you gripe all the time about it? It's horrible and I'm tired of it.

SHE: I said I'll stop.

HE: It's depressing to hear the same complaints over and over again.

Dialogue 1—Constructive

SHE: God, I hate going to work.

HE: I know you've been unhappy with the job for several months. What are you going to do about it?

Notice that in the constructive response the man first acknowledges the complaint but then focuses on *future* actions rather than belaboring the past. The fact that she has complained about her job in the past is important only in that it tells him it is more than a momentary reaction. Realizing this, he attempts to get her to think about ways of resolving her dilemma. What the person in the first dialogue does not realize is that his continual criticism of the woman's complaints may indeed prompt her to stop complaining but will also elicit resentment toward him.

Dialogue 2—Destructive

HE: If you had begun getting dressed earlier, we wouldn't have been late. Now we'll be the last ones there, and it's an important dinner party.

SHE: I'm sorry. I didn't think it would take this long to get there.

HE: Well, you should have known. If we were going somewhere *you* wanted to go, you would have been ready much earlier.

SHE: I'm sorry. Why don't we just forget it and have a good time?

(Later)

SHE: That sure was a nice party. I had a good time, didn't you?

HE: I would've had a better time if we had gotten there on time. You ruined it for me by making us late.

SHE: I said I was sorry.

HE: You're always sorry.

Dialogue 2—Constructive

HE: I wish you had begun getting dressed earlier. Now it looks like we'll be late.

SHE: I'm sorry. I didn't realize it would take this long.

HE: Next time, when I tell you it's an important dinner party, I'd appreciate it if you could get started earlier.

SHE: OK. I promise.

HE: Well, we can't do anything about it now, so let's forget it and have a good time.

In each of these examples of constructive criticism, one principle was implied but deserves special attention. It concerns the tendency to level accusations at people whose actions, lack of actions, mistakes or comments bother us. It is as if we are saying, "Since you hurt me, I will now get my revenge by hurting you." But these accusations invariably evolve into a meaningless battle, with each person defending his own position. To avoid this problem, tell the person how his behavior or words affected *you* personally. In so doing you are more likely to engage the individual in a constructive dialogue and to obtain his cooperation in resolving the problem. Consider the difference in tone and words between the following accusatory comment and a constructive alternative concerning the same issue.

Accusatory Comment: "You don't care about anything anymore except your job."

Constructive Alternative: "Since you started working, I feel neglected."

Two elements make this last statement constructive. First, the conditions that create the disturbing feeling are stated clearly ("Since you started working...."), leaving no room for guessing games about when the problem began. Second, the phrase "I feel" conveys a personal reaction, which you are entitled to have and which cannot be disputed. The accusatory comment, on the other hand, can easily lead to a "Yes, I do—No, you don't" argument, which is fruitless.

Other nonjudgmental phrases can also convey information on *your* emotional reactions to the other person's shortcomings, actions, lack of actions, or statements:

- "I get upset when you _____."
- "It makes me angry when you _____."
- "I am confused by your lack of _____."
- "When you do ___ (or don't do ___) I feel that you don't care."

In short, what you emphasize makes the difference in how your message comes across.

Here are three more examples, concerning different issues, of accusatory comments with constructive alternatives:

Accusatory Comment: "You constantly ignore my requests."

Constructive Alternative: "When I ask you several times to do something, and it doesn't get done, I feel ignored."

Accusatory Comment: "You don't care what I think about how we spend our money."

Constructive Alternative: "When it comes to spending money, I get the feeling that my opinion doesn't matter to you."

Accusatory Comment: "Your career is the only thing that matters to you."

Constructive Alternative: "When you spend sixty hours at work and then bring work home with you, I feel I'm not as important to you as your job."

In the above examples, emphasizing *your* feelings and the effect your spouse's actions has on you to some extent prevents your spouse from responding defensively. Furthermore, the likelihood that the two of you will discuss the problem rationally increases.

Finally, when offering criticism it is advisable to introduce your complaint with a positive or favorable statement about your spouse. Remember, "a spoonful of sugar helps the medicine go down." For example, say "I'm glad to meet your friends, but I wish next time you'd give me notice before you invite them for dinner," or "You really look nice, but those shoes don't go with the dress." In short, criticism is much better received when it is preceded by a compliment.

Let's summarize the major principles of criticism by presenting some common situations in which criticism is warranted and then suggesting appropriate ways of offering the criticism.

Situation: When you were at a party with your spouse, he said something that embarrassed you. Later, when the two of you are alone, you say:

Suggested Response: "That was a nice party. But, I must tell you that it upset me when you said ___ . Before you say things about me to others, I'd appreciate it if you'd think about how your comment will affect me."

Situation: Your spouse has just told you he purchased an expensive item that will be delivered in a few days. You believe you should have been consulted before he made the purchase. You say:

Suggested Response: "I'm angry that you didn't consult me before you bought it. Don't I have anything to say about whether we should spend this money?" (Wait for a response and then tell him that next time you want a say in such important matters.)

Situation: Your spouse bought you a gift that you did not like. You say:

Suggested Response: "That was really thoughtful of you to buy me a gift. I really appreciate the thought, but I hope you don't mind if I exchange it since it's not quite what I like."

AVOIDING GUESSING GAMES

You may be familiar with a game children play, which goes something like this: One youngster says to another, "I know something you don't know, and I bet you can't guess what it is." The victim, who is now baited by curiosity, assumes the secret is about her and is probably bad. Hoping she will accurately guess the secret, she inadvertently confesses to some real or imagined misdemeanors or indiscretions. After fully taxing her imagination and being told that none of her guesses were correct, the victim gives up in desperation. The initiator of this game may, at this point, choose to reveal what she knows or may walk away, saying, "I can't tell you."

The adult variation of this game is considerably more sophisticated but just as cruel. Those who initiate it do so with a vague statement that triggers the victim's imagination. In so doing, they maintain control over the person by keeping him guessing, allowing him to imagine the worst. Such games are counterproductive to a healthy marriage partnership.

Suppose your sour facial expression prompts your spouse to ask, "What's wrong?" You reply, "Nothing," when in fact you are bothered by something. The contradiction of your verbal response by your facial expression is confusing. So he persists by asking, "Then why the sour look?" You reply, "It's nothing important."

This vague response can mean several things to your spouse:

1. There *is* something wrong, and it probably involves me. (What did I do now?)
2. There *is* something wrong, but she doesn't want me to know. (What secret is she keeping from me?)
3. There *is* something wrong, but it has nothing to do with me. (So why can't I be told?)
4. There *is* something wrong, but she doesn't want to talk about it now. (How long will I be held in suspense?)
5. There is really *nothing* wrong. (So why the sour look?)

Your spouse's response to "nothing" will, of course, depend on how he interprets it. Chances are, however, that he will imagine the worst, become defensive (or offensive) and then angry or withdrawn.

Wouldn't it be more forthright to say, "Yes there is something bothering me, but it has nothing to do with you; I'll talk to you about it later tonight," or "Yes, there is something bothering me, but I'd prefer to discuss it after dinner (or when we're alone)." Regardless of your response, the point is that you *must not be so evasive that your spouse imagines things that can create barriers or misunderstandings.*

Honesty is not *always* the best policy, but forthrightness is. When you are vague or nonspecific as opposed to being forthright about important matters, you are flirting with danger, as is evident in the following example.

HE: I want to talk to you tonight.
SHE: Is it about something good or bad?
HE: Never mind. You'll find out soon enough.
SHE: Can't you at least tell me what it's about?
HE: I don't want to discuss it now.

Whether or not he realizes it, the man is placing the woman in a defensive posture. What would you think if you were on the receiving end of his game? He would have been more forthright if he had said, "It's not a matter of good or bad, but rather a problem that concerns me. Please respect my desire not to discuss it now. I just mentioned it so you don't make plans to do anything until after we've talked."

Here is another example of the same problem.

SHE: Did you get the gift I sent you?
HE: Yes I did.
SHE: Did you like it?
HE: I appreciate the thought.

Did he like it or not? If he liked it, why didn't he say so? If he didn't like it, maybe it could be exchanged for another gift. What would you think if you were the woman in this dialogue? Assuming he didn't like it, a more forthright response would have been, "I appreciate the thought, but it's not anything I can use. Could I exchange it?" or "It's very nice, but it doesn't suit me," or simply "It's very nice, thank you." The last comment is not necessarily dishonest, since it is nice for *someone*.

While these "games" are not necessarily intended to be harmful, they nevertheless create unproductive tension within the person whose questions or concerns are unresolved. Waiting for a decision, a response to a request, an expected phone call, an explanation of an action or reaction, or any information that is important to the individual is painful. That pain intensifies the longer one has to wait for such information. Even if you are the bearer of unpleasant news, it would be kinder to present it as soon as possible than to create unnecessary tensions. Most people are able to handle unpleasant news or disappointment much better than they can deal with uncertainty.

HEALTHY VERSUS UNHEALTHY ASSUMPTIONS

Our attitudes, actions, and reactions toward others are influenced and guided by the assumptions we make about them. While you may not always be conscious of your assumptions, your demeanor in every waking moment suggests their presence. For instance, it goes without saying that I wouldn't have written this book if I had not thought that a publisher would buy it. You and I assume we will be compensated for whatever services we offer to others. We also assume that all people are not out to cheat us, that we will be punished if we commit a crime, that the person who is driving the car alongside ours on the freeway will not ram into us, that our parents love us, etc. Without these and all the other assumptions we make we would be immobile.

Our assumptions may prove to be true or false; they may also be healthy or unhealthy. What frequently gets people into trouble is when making *false* assumptions and acting as if they are true. Suppose, for example, that you assumed your spouse would be responsive to your needs and desires, regardless of how poorly you treated him. This assumption is called a *false positive* because you *wrongly* assumed that a favorable outcome would result from your actions. In making this false positive assumption you would be guilty of taking your spouse for granted and, in so doing, create feelings of resentment. The fact is that any consideration you want from people, including your spouse, has to be earned.

People who make false positive assumptions are optimistic. However, their optimism is not based on reality. They will spend money they don't have in the hope that something good will happen to alter their financial state. They will make commitments that include others in hopes that these people will say "yes." And, they will celebrate the *promise* of a promotion, assuming it *will* happen. Because many of their positive assumptions turn out to be false, they frequently are disappointed and become disillusioned with people and even with life.

False negative assumptions, which are incorrect beliefs that other people's motives, interests, or desires are at odds with yours, lead to misunderstandings and destructive arguments. People who make such assumptions wrongly believe that others are out to hurt them, that others will not be responsive to their needs or desires, that others don't really care about them, and that most people are guilty until they prove themselves innocent. Convinced that the qualities and motives they impute to others are true, these people tend to make false accusations, become needlessly resentful and angry, and are constantly on the defensive. In their effort to protect themselves from the "enemy," they fail to enjoy relationships that could otherwise be satisfying.

Still another tendency of people who make false negative assumptions is their reluctance either to offer their services to others or to ask them for anything, including their time, if there is the slightest chance of rejection. Rather than take that risk, they merely opt for a safer alternative.

Consider the following dialogue as a case in point.

HE: I'm going to the Bulls' basketball game with Joe this Friday.

SHE: Why with Joe?

HE: I got two free tickets, so I asked him to join me.

SHE: Why didn't you ask me?

HE: I didn't think you wanted to go. I know you don't enjoy basketball that much. Frankly, I thought of asking you, but I figured you'd say no.

SHE: You're right; basketball doesn't turn me on. But I would have gone so we could be together. You had no business deciding for me that I didn't want to go. Next time would you *ask* me instead of making my decisions for me?

Her point obviously is well taken. What is the worst thing that could have happened had he asked her to accompany him? Had she said "no" he still could have asked Joe. By failing to honor her right to make her own decisions, he not only angered her but also led her to believe that perhaps he prefers Joe's company to hers.

Here is another problem created by a false negative assumption.

SHE: I had a ton of things to do today that required a lot of running around, but there was no one to help me.

HE: Why didn't you ask me to help you? I could have done some of those errands.

SHE: I didn't want to bother you because I thought you were busy.

HE: I *was* busy, but I still could have taken some time out to give you a hand. Rather than see you upset, I would have helped you. All you had to do was ask.

SHE: I thought you'd be upset if I asked.

HE: Do me a favor. Don't make decisions for me. If you want something from me, ask; if I can't do it, I'll tell you.

Let's examine some common *unhealthy* negative assumptions that people make about their marriage partners as well as their *healthy* counterparts.

Unhealthy
Assumption: *My spouse really doesn't care about my feelings.*

When your desires and needs are not fulfilled or when your expectations are not met, this belief can easily lead to accusations. It also can cause you to misinterpret constructive criticisms and ent, consider them personal affronts. Even innocplayful gibes may be taken the wrong way.

Healthy
Assumption: *My spouse really cares about my feelings and would not deliberately hurt or upset me.*

This assumption enables you to overlook or tolerate your spouse's minor idiosyncrasies, which normally irritate you. Giving your partner the benefit of your doubts, you would not make a major issue of an *occasional* thoughtless comment or action. You would assume that other factors, having nothing to do with you, prompted this behavior or insensitive remark.

Unhealthy
Assumption: *My spouse is my competitor.*

Win-lose situations, with each person trying to "put down" or gain dominance over the other, can be expected when you hold to this assumption. In a competitive relationship one person must emerge triumphant at the expense of the other. Such power struggles in marriage only weaken the relationship.

Healthy
Assumption: *My spouse is my partner.*

Cooperation and helpful, supportive actions come naturally when couples share this belief. Partners realize that complementing, rather than belittling and fighting each other, is the only way to build a healthy relationship. They also know that by helping their partner they benefit themselves.

Unhealthy
Assumption: *My spouse is my possession.*

People who are viewed as possessions are treated as *things*, not as humans. You buy things, use them as needed, and then put them aside when they are not needed. No person I know likes to be treated in this fashion.

Healthy
Assumption: *My spouse is a unique and special person, not an object.*

Because people have feelings and thoughts, they want to be treated with respect and dignity. Their importance, at least in their own eyes, extends beyond their functional value. Most people will not tolerate others who treat them as objects.

Unhealthy

Assumption: *Regardless of how I treat my spouse, he will not desert me.*

This false assumption is probably the single most common cause of marital conflict. As stated earlier, nobody likes to be taken for granted. Those who believe they are may feel justified in seeking other relationships that will support their feelings of self-worth.

Healthy

Assumption: *I must earn my spouse's loyalty.*

When you assume that loyalty is not coming to you but must be earned, you will tend to be considerate of your partner's needs and desires. Through your actions you will communicate the feeling that she is an important and special person in your life.

Unhealthy

Assumption: *We must have exactly the same interests.*

If you hold to this belief, you might become resentful when your spouse does not participate actively in your hobbies or in your areas of interest. Even if your spouse shared *all* of your interests, at the risk of not having any of his own, there is a strong possibility that your range of conversation would be limited and, therefore, you might become bored with each other.

Healthy

Assumption: *Being an individual, my spouse is entitled to interests different from mine.*

Important as it is to have a few interests that captivate both of you, your individuality demands expression through your own hobbies and interests. While you might initially believe that your divergent interests will put more distance between you, the fact is they can vitalize your relationship.

Unhealthy
Assumption: *I can't discuss disturbing thoughts and important issues with my spouse.*

Whatever your reasons for not sharing disturbing thoughts and feelings with your spouse, your unwillingness to take this risk can invite trouble, particularly if your spouse finds out about them later. If you remember that partners help each other, you must be willing to invite that help by airing your concerns.

Healthy
Assumption: *Telling my spouse what is troubling me cannot possibly be as bad as the feeling I experience when I keep these thoughts inside.*

This belief enables you to be forthright with your spouse and honest with yourself; it also provides you with one of the major benefits of a marriage partnership. Being free to discuss your disturbing feelings relieves the pressures those feelings create and increases the chances for resolving your problems, which may involve your spouse. While the very consequences of being forthright that you fear *could* occur, a realistic resolution is possible only when you face those fears squarely. However, if you believe that sharing your disturbing feelings will hurt your spouse deeply, and may even be damaging to your relationship, you might consider keeping them to yourself or discussing them with a professional.

Because actions and reactions are influenced by your assumptions, making adverse assumptions that prove to be false can be harmful to your relationship. You can avoid the danger of making false adverse assumptions by employing any one or a combination of the following three suggestions.

First, verify your assumptions; get the facts. If, for example, you are uncertain of the exact meaning behind your partner's actions or reactions, *ask*. Obtain the information you need to fully understand the intended meaning of a message. Questions such as the following are some ways to check your assumptions.

- "Is there a reason why you said _____?"
- "What did you mean when you said _____?"
- "When you did _____ , what did you have in mind?"
- "What you did baffled me. What did you hope to accomplish?"

The more information you have, the better equipped you are to react appropriately.

Second, tell your partner how you interpret the message so that she can correct you if you have misunderstood. Statements such as those below will let her know that you want to determine the accuracy of your assumptions. (Notice that these are not judgmental statements.)

- "Are you saying _____?"
- "What I hear you saying is _____."
- "From your actions it appears to me that _____."

Finally, don't make your assumptions sound like accusations. Rather, state them as beliefs, which is all they are until they have been substantiated. The statements and questions that follow give the other person an opportunity to disagree with you if your assumptions are incorrect.

- "Can I assume from your actions that _____?"
- "I assume from what you're saying that _____."

- "Can I conclude from your comment that _____?"

Accusations only close the door to a meaningful interchange. They convey a feeling of self-righteousness and make it clear that you are not willing to discuss the matter.

In addition to these three suggestions, whenever possible, it's a good practice to make positive rather than negative assumptions, since the wounds created by false adverse accusations are difficult to heal. Here are a few ways to give your spouse the benefit of your doubts:

- "I'm sure you didn't mean to hurt me when you _____."
- "You must have been awfully busy not to call me all day."
- "I don't think you intended to insult me, but _____."
- "I know you're under pressure, and that's why you _____."

If, however, your positive assumptions prove incorrect, you can present a stronger argument to support your criticism with evidence to back you up.

Before concluding this discussion, we must consider one other possibility. Suppose one or several of the unhealthy assumptions we discussed earlier are not assumptions at all but are actually facts. The only way to handle this problem is to confront your spouse with your concerns. The following examples of opening statements are some ways to introduce your concerns.

- "It seems to me that my feelings are not important to you. For example, _____ (give evidence to support your position)."
- "Why do we have to have exactly the same interests?"
- "Why do I get the feeling that I can't discuss with you things that bother me?"
- "Why is it that we have to compete with each other for things we both want or need?"

The discussion that will follow, assuming you employ the other communication guidelines presented here, should lead to a constructive resolution. The next chapter, on how to resolve conflicts constructively, will provide you with additional insights into dealing with conflicts.

"WHY" QUESTIONS—WHEN AND WHEN NOT TO ASK THEM

"Why" questions are tricky. Depending on one's reasons for asking them, they can either pave the way for better understanding between two people or trigger a defensive and possible hostile reaction. Let us first consider the value such questions have. Suppose you are upset because your spouse did not phone you when she promised. Rather than verbally attacking her when she finally does call, you assume that there must have been a good reason for failing to keep her promise. So, you ask in a pleasant tone of voice, "Why didn't you call me like you said you would?" This "why" question is a legitimate request for information which, when answered, may temper your anger. After all, there may indeed be a valid reason she did not phone you when she said she would, and you owe it to yourself and to her to determine the reason.

Knowing the reason why something was or was not said or done helps you formulate an appropriate reaction. You are less likely to jump to the wrong conclusion if you understand fully the circumstances and motivations that prompt a person's behavior. That information may even suggest ways you can help him respond more appropriately, and to your liking, to similar circumstances that arise in the future.

This is illustrated in the following dialogue that occurred after this couple came home from visiting some friends. Notice that the "why" question, which concerns a thoughtless act, also stimulates him to think rationally about his actions.

SHE: Why did you belittle me tonight?
HE: I did what?

SHE: You belittled me when you told them that I exaggerate about the importance of my job.

HE: I didn't mean to belittle you.

SHE: Well, if you didn't mean to do it, next time I say something that you don't agree with, tell me privately. Don't insult me in front of others.

HE: I'm sorry. I really didn't mean to.

Because he is sincerely interested in her explanation, and she accepts his apology, this "why" question leads to a constructive resolution of the problem.

While "why" questions can generate valuable information, they frequently are used as smoke screens to corner a person and make him squirm. Other times they are merely disguised criticisms or they are used as prefaces to criticism. In these cases the questions are invariably rhetorical. After all, how does one respond to dead-end questions such as these?

- "Why did you do such a dumb thing?"
- "Why did you buy such an ugly outfit?"
- "Why did you act so stupid?"

These "why" questions are not really legitimate requests for information. Rather, they are examples of verbal abuse couched in a question. To interpret such questions literally, one would have to admit to being thoughtless, naive, and indiscreet, which would then open the door for further abuse. Obviously the only response to such "questions" is to say nothing, allowing the critic to say whatever he has to say.

When you are upset about something your spouse said, did, or did not say or do, and no explanation will appease you, don't ask for one. Rather, tell her how you would prefer she handle the same situation in the future. You can let her know you are angry, and not interested in reasons or excuses, without pinning her against the wall. Some examples are:

- "I'd appreciate it if you wouldn't open my mail."

- "I wish you'd be more considerate of my feelings."
- "If you know in advance that you can't help me, I wish you wouldn't make such promises."

One final point: If your spouse asks you one of these disguised "why" questions, and you believe it is not a sincere request for information, handle it as you would an emotional reaction or criticism.

CHOICES—WHEN AND WHEN NOT TO GIVE THEM

When you give someone a choice or ask for his preference, that person rightfully assumes that you will accede to his desire. Unfortunately, that assumption is not necessarily correct. Frequently, people give others choices or ask for their opinions when all they really want is an affirmation of their own decision. Under such conditions, offering choices or asking for opinions is deceptive, dishonest, and manipulative. It is a setup that can easily deteriorate into a communication breakdown. Those who are guilty of such manipulations want to appear fair and open-minded, when actually they are not.

An employer once asked me, "How much of a salary increase do you think you should receive?" Interpreting this question as a legitimate request for my opinion, I quoted what I thought was a fair figure. He replied, "Our budget allows for a maximum 5 percent raise; that is all we can give you."

"If you knew this in advance, why did you ask me?" I responded. "Apparently what *I* thought didn't really matter."

"That's true," he replied. "But we want our employees to feel that we are interested in their opinions."

His question, which proved to be insincere, demonstrated his lack of integrity and therefore reduced his credibility. Following this incident, I was suspicious of his motives whenever he asked my opinion on anything.

When you are set in your ideas, and there is no room for

discussion, inform your spouse of your desires, preferences, or what you are able to offer, rather than railroading her into a decision you've already made. To illustrate, here are two dialogues. The first is certain to create resentment; the second is a more forthright approach.

A Manipulative Approach

HE: Where would you like to go tonight?
SHE: How about going to a movie?
HE: I don't feel like going to a movie.
SHE: OK. How about going out to dinner?
HE: We always go out to dinner. No, I don't want to do that.
SHE: Well, what would *you* like to do?
HE: It makes no difference to me; whatever you want is fine.
SHE: Should I call the Smiths and ask them if they want to come over for a while?
HE: I'm really not in the mood for being with people tonight and making small talk.
SHE: Well, then, why don't we just stay home and watch TV?
HE: That sounds good.
SHE: That's what you wanted to do all along, wasn't it?
HE: Yeah, but I thought I'd ask you anyway.

A Forthright Approach

HE: I'm really not in the mood for doing anything special tonight. How about staying home?
SHE: OK. Maybe we can go out tomorrow night.
HE: Fine.

A major problem in giving someone a choice is that it creates expectations. In the first dialogue, for example, by asking, "Where would you like to go tonight?" the man creates a desire that starts the creative juices flowing. As the woman thinks of possibilities, the desire to go out for the evening is intensified. What a letdown it must be when she realizes that the original question was insincere.

Here is another example:

A Manipulative Approach

SHE: Do you want me to call your folks or do you want to?
HE: Would you call them?
SHE: But they're your parents. Why should I call them?
HE: I thought you gave me a choice.
SHE: I'm always doing your work for you. It's not my job to call them. If you want to talk to them, you call.

A Forthright Approach

SHE: You haven't talked with your parents in over a month; I think it would be nice if you called them.
HE: I'm not in the mood to call them now; maybe tomorrow.
SHE: Well, I just thought I'd remind you.

LEGITIMATE PRIDE VERSUS FALSE PRIDE

Picture this. You and your spouse are driving someplace you've never been to before. It suddenly occurs to both of you that you're lost. Spotting a gas station, your spouse says, "Let's go in there and ask for directions." To which you reply, "I don't have to ask for directions; I'll find my way."

Why the resistance in asking for help? The culprit is pride—
false pride. It is one of the major obstacles to getting what we
want from others and for ourselves.

There is an important difference, however, between false pride
and legitimate pride. Legitimate pride is the good feeling you get
from maintaining standards of excellence, achieving your objectives, fulfilling promises to yourself and others, and aiming for
performance that comes up to your capabilities. The truly proud
person does not permit himself to be sidetracked from realizing
his objectives.

Achieving worthwhile objectives, and feeling good about
doing so, are not the prime concerns of people who exhibit false
pride. These individuals are interested mostly in protecting and
perpetuating whatever image they have of themselves and wish to
project to others.

In our mind's eye, all of us have a complex, multidimensional
picture of ourselves. That picture is portrayed to others through
characteristic behavior, which also reinforces our view of ourselves. If, for example, a person sees himself as a "macho man,"
there are certain things he will and will not do to convince others
and himself that this self-image is genuine.

In addition to having this complex image of ourselves, we also
have strong beliefs about how people in certain roles or bearing
certain labels should or should not behave. These personal "rules
of conduct" dictate our activities and reactions when we or others
fit one of these roles. For example, we all follow our own rules of
conduct when acting in our roles as husband, wife, parent, friend,
professional, son, daughter, etc. And we impute these rules to
others who occupy these positions. We also have private beliefs
about what it means to be strong, weak, masculine, feminine,
honest, ambitious, lazy, and so on.

While it is essential to portray a self-image you feel comfortable
with, and to adopt rules of conduct for each role you occupy,
when these portrayals and rules interfere with accomplishing
more vital objectives you are guilty of *false* pride.

Admittedly, when you ask for help, apologize, admit to being
wrong, express your feeings, and do things that you feel are

beneath you, you risk losing face. Isn't it worth taking that risk if in so doing you can fulfill tangible and meaningful objectives? Let's look at an example.

Suppose a wife, who normally does the dishes, asks her husband to do them because she either is not feeling well or has had a tiring day. He would view her request as a threat to his masculine image if he felt that household chores were "women's work." While he would feel justified in rejecting her request, he would disregard three objectives that are far more important than perpetuating his image: (1) to let her know, through his actions, that he is sensitive to her feelings and temporary condition, (2) to do his part in maintaining an orderly house, and (3) to avert a possible argument concerning his lack of sensitivity to her condition. If he were to reject her request, he would indeed uphold his masculine image, but at a costly price.

When faced with two possible courses of action, one of which might jeopardize your self-image, ask yourself, "What are my most important objectives?" More often than not, your response will direct you to a decision that will be more satisfying than maintaining your image.

The following two dialogues demonstrate the fruitlessness of false pride:

Dialogue 1

HE: We're in a financial bind; I don't know how we're going to get out of it.
SHE: I'll get a job.
HE: No wife of mine will work.
SHE: But it will only be for a short while, until we can get out of this mess.
HE: You're just trying to prove that I'm not a good provider.
SHE: No, I just want to help.
HE: I don't need your help; I'll work out the problem myself.

Dialogue 2

HE: Hasn't it been a year since you've had your last raise?
SHE: It's been over a year, and I'm really angry.
HE: So why don't you ask her (the manager) about it?
SHE: I refuse to beg for something I deserve. I have done a good
job; I shouldn't have to ask her for a raise.
HE: But maybe she forgot.
SHE: I don't care. If I have to ask her, she can stuff it.

In both these instances, who are the losers? Obviously, it's those
who fail to get what is *really* important.

Exhibiting false pride—failing to ask for help or rejecting it
when you really need it, failing to apologize when you are in the
wrong, or refusing to make the first move toward reconciliation
after a falling out with your spouse—can deprive you of things
that are more vital than your self-image. The point is that in most
instances it doesn't matter what others think of you if, in the end,
you benefit and no one is harmed by your actions. Actually, it is a
sign of strength and character to concern yourself with objectives
that *really* count rather than to worry about your image.

ACTIONS VERSUS WORDS: WHICH ARE MOST IMPORTANT?

"Seeing is believing," "actions speak louder than words," and
"put your money where your mouth is," are common phrases
that remind us of the limitations of words. Be they promises,
statements of desires, or expressions of feelings, words are empty
unless they are reinforced with actions. Why? Because actions are
real in that they require effort, time, and sometimes money; they
give substance and meaning to words. Words are nothing more
than symbols that create images of the real world.

Because all of us are insecure to some degree, we need reassurance that other people's words are sincere. Particularly in intimate relationships, we need as much evidence as possible to convince ourselves that we are loved. *Saying* nice things to your partner without backing them up with action creates a credibility gap. On the other hand, when you do things that you know are important to your spouse (without violating your self-respect), your actions say, "I'm thinking of you; I care about you; I love you."

Just as words have to be backed up with appropriate actions, actions often must be supported by words. Actions, for instance, can be ambiguous and therefore are susceptible to misinterpretation. You may recall the song, "Do You Love Me?" from *Fiddler on the Roof*. The hero, Tevye, asks his wife, "Do you love me?" Rather than answering his questions directly, she relates all the things she has done for him: for twenty-five years she has cooked for him, cleaned for him, had his children, etc. She finally concludes, "If that isn't love, what is?" But Tevye isn't satisfied. He wants to hear her say, "I love you," because it's quite possible that his wife's actions were motivated by obligation rather than love. Words can also stimulate certain emotional and intellectual senses that actions alone do not. Together, however, actions and words convey a convincing, forceful message.

MANAGING IMPULSIVE REACTIONS

Getting things off your chest, telling your spouse off, or saying other hurtful things in anger may make you feel good temporarily, but the long-range consequences can be devastating. Such impulsive reactions can be minimized by asking yourself, "What value would be gained by saying or doing __?" If your answer is, "Nothing," *keep quiet until your emotional impulse passes.* It takes only a fraction of a second to ask yourself this question, which gives you just enough time to think before you react.

This does not mean that you keep your anger bottled up. Rather, temper your impulses so that you can express your anger constructively in the manner suggested earlier. Asking yourself, "What value would be gained by _____?" will aid you in collecting your thoughts so you don't say or do something you'll regret later.

If you find yourself on the receiving end of an impulsive reaction, with your spouse letting off steam or complaining, chances are she is not at all interested in what you have to say about whatever is bothering her. All she wants is to vent her feelings. Under these conditions it is best to remain silent and assume a passive-receptive posture, since nothing you can say at such times would make any difference to her. The fact is that *not every statement your spouse utters, whether or not it is in anger, warrants a response.*

If you have a reaction to something and need to express it, wait until your spouse is more receptive before you respond. To say anything when your partner is emotionally wrapped up with himself would add fuel to an existing fire. Admittedly, it takes self-control to be silent rather than to react to tirades, nonstop complaints, or a soul-baring monologue. But consider the benefits of this strategy.

2

Resolving Conflicts Constructively

CONFLICTS and arguments occur in the best of marriages. Even if you were to practice all the principles presented here, you and your spouse could not avoid conflicts. Couples who claim they never argue are not only deluding themselves, but they most likely do not have a healthy relationship. You will and must have differences if your marriage is to be interesting and dynamic. However, your arguments need not be destructive.

Let's consider five *legitimate* causes of conflicts as well as constructive approaches for resolving them.

PRESSURES—SELF-CREATED AND IMPOSED

The fast pace and demands of modern living create many

pressures. Some can be so overwhelming that they drain you of the emotional resources necessary to be as understanding, considerate, and loving as you would like to be. A bad day at work, a rough day with the children, a major disappointment, and other stresses of daily living can wear on your emotions.

When you are emotionally or intellectually drained, other people, including your spouse, become burdens. Therefore, any request your partner makes of you is either blown out of proportion or regarded as unimportant. An innocent comment may trigger an unreasonable reaction. Being pleasant becomes a chore. All you want is to be left alone. While this attitude is perfectly understandable under stressful conditions, it can precipitate a battle if not handled properly.

Look at it from your partner's point of view. He has no way of knowing that you are emotionally vulnerable or that you are on edge unless you tell him. You must inform (or warn) him, as quickly as possible, that you've had a tough day and may not be civil. You must also tell him that you need a little time to yourself to "recharge your batteries" and to regain your composure. You must tell him all this so that he won't inadvertently push you over the brink or expect things from you that you are unable to give at the moment.

By informing your spouse early of your emotional state, before any serious interchange occurs, you are saying in effect, "My nerves are shot, so just let me be until I'm ready to face the world again." A simple statement such as, "It's been a rough day; I'll tell you about it later," or "I need to be alone for about a half-hour" should set the stage for the peace and quiet you need to settle down.

When *you* are told by your spouse that she has had a rough day, back off until you receive a signal that all is OK. Do not, under any circumstances, humor her or underplay her bad mood. That simply makes it worse, since she will probably misinterpret your intentions and respond angrily. Most people don't like to be humored when they are in a bad mood. They need to work it out themselves.

Occasionally, both of you will have an emotionally draining

day. When that happens you have to decide between you who is hurting more at the moment. If you don't have small children, it's easy: you simply go your separate ways until all is well. But, if you have children to consider, you will have to take turns. Deciding who goes first will again depend on which of you has the greatest need to unwind.

YOUR PHYSICAL CONDITION

Just as job and domestic pressures affect a person's emotional state, so does the way one feels physically. When you are tired or do not feel well your perceptions of people and the world around you become somewhat distorted. You tend to be more sensitive than usual, and minor disturbances or problems become magnified. Chances are that anything your spouse says or does will irritate you, and your reactions will reflect that irritation. What your spouse may not realize is that your anger probably has very little, if anything, to do with his behavior.

When you are under the weather, you owe it to your partner to tell him. In so doing you alert him to the possibility that you will be less than reasonable. Being aware of how you feel, he is more likely to tolerate your impatience and irritability. Saying, "I'm not feeling well," or "I'm very tired," or "I'm feeling lousy" serves as a warning signal. If your spouse insists on taking offense, make it clear in whatever way you can that he is not the cause of your irritations.

If your spouse is the one who is edgy and unreasonable, and you suspect that he may not be feeling well (although he hasn't said so), you can save yourself aggravation by asking: "Is it me you're upset with, or aren't you feeling well?" His answer will, of course, determine your next response. If he is upset about something you said or did, proceed to resolve the problem, utilizing the principles you have learned so far, plus those contained in the rest of this section.

PERSONALITY DIFFERENCES

While our unique personalities make us interesting to each other, major conflicts can arise when couples are too different in certain respects. Let's consider, for example, what happens when a highly sensitive person is married to one who is extremely insensitive.

Highly sensitive, thin-skinned individuals are easily offended, disappointed, and angered because they insist on reading more into a statement, question, or action than is actually intended by the other person. For example, a statement such as, "I don't have time to talk to you now," may be interpreted by thin-skinned people as: "You're not very important to me." Similarly, casual questions, oversights, and unintentional, thoughtless actions are viewed by sensitive individuals as personal affronts and criticisms. In short, because highly sensitive people tend to be overly *self*-critical, they make more than their fair share of false negative assumptions concernng other people's motives.

On the other end of the scale are the highly insensitive people who typically minimize the importance of, or are impervious to, others' feelings or desires. Being thick-skinned, they are oblivious to subtle cries for help, as well as to the emotional elements of messages directed toward them. They tend to view things strictly from a rational point of view. Oblivious of other people's feelings, they do not realize that they are hurting them deeply when they tell them off, ignore them, or insult them. However, they are angered and deeply hurt when their own feelings are injured. Having a double standard, they are sensitive to their own feelings but insensitive to those of others.

If a wide difference in sensitivity exists between you, even if it is not as extreme as described here, you can minimize your conflicts by changing your attitudes.

The following attitudes must be adopted by the *more* sensitive spouse.

1. Knowing yourself as you do, you will be aware when your

sensitivity is interfering with your perceptions. Rather than jumping to conclusions, apply the techniques discussed earlier under the heading, "Healthy versus Unhealthy Assumptions" (p. 27). Once you realize that much of what you call sensitivity is nothing more than false assumptions in action, you can help yourself become less critical of yourself and others.

2. Don't sit back and let yourself be hurt by your sensitivity. Tell your spouse what you are actually hearing or feeling, i.e., how his messages are coming through to you. Then, when he corrects himself or clarifies his *real* intentions, realize that your perceptions are unfounded.

3. Believe the corrected version of what your spouse said or did; don't harp on what you *thought* she meant. Sincerely believe that your partner would not *deliberately* hurt or offend you.

The *less* sensitive spouse must adopt the following attitudes.

1. Accept the fact that your spouse has a fragile ego that has to be handled with care. Her fragile ego doesn't make her bad or good; it's just part of her nature. While you may not like this quality in her, you have to learn to live with and adjust to it, just as she must live with and adjust to your peculiarities. Furthermore, rather than considering this characteristic a major problem and a burden, think of it as an unchangeable quality that makes her the person she is—a quality that has its charms as well as its drawbacks.

2. When you feel you are misunderstood (and you will be), take extra effort to clarify what you *really* mean. Remember, if a statement, question, or action can be taken two ways (and most can), your sensitive spouse will probably assume the worst. Be patient.

3. Loving your spouse as you do, respect his sensitivity by taking time to allay his concerns and doubts. Offer whatever clarifications or explanations are necessary to assure your spouse that you truly love him. Lots of tender, loving care and attention is what your sensitive partner needs from you. Realize that in addition to having a fragile ego, your spouse has a hungry one.

DIFFERENCES IN VALUES

Couples may, and frequently do, disagree on how problems or situations should be handled, on how to use their available time and money, and on the meaning or ramifications of an event or a set of facts. These differences reflect their individual values.

Because values are strongly held beliefs that are deeply ingrained in each of us, we tend to defend them, sometimes at the cost of alienating someone who doesn't share those values. When conflict between values arises, the immediate response usually is, "He is wrong and I am right." This position can easily lead to major conflict and lose-lose battles.

While you should not abdicate your values, you can resolve your differences by adopting a win-win attitude. Asking yourself, "What can I say or do, and what concessions can I make, to reach some sort of mutually agreeable course of action?" will enable you to come up with workable solutions. That attitude—namely, "How can we both win, without either of us sacrificing our values?"—has to be foremost in your mind if you are to resolve these major differences.

Realize that disagreements, even those that concern values, are not invitations to hurt or destroy your spouse. They are not opportunities to prove your superiority. They are not occasions to demonstrate your power over your spouse. Rather, they are challenges to your ability to reach an understanding and a decision both of you can live with. Neither false pride nor rigidity has a place in reaching a mutually agreeable decision or course of action.

Before going over some specific suggestions for negotiating your differences in values, let us review a crucial concept discussed earlier. As you know, emotions are brainless. When you are highly emotional, your sense of reason is dulled and the "filtering mechanism" in your brain does not function well. Under these conditions you will say and do things you may later regret. Furthermore, you will be closed to new ideas and might even consider them threatening. When that happens your chances of working out your differences are poor.

If you have ever tried to argue with someone who is upset, angry, or emotionally tied to a particular belief, you know that logic and reason do not work. But that should be understandable. After all, everyone sometimes does something that *feels* good even though the action makes no sense. And there are times when we all dread doing something even though we *know* it will be good for us. Let's face it, the emotional forces within us frequently overpower our sense of logic, despite the fact that we like to view ourselves as rational human beings.

Since feelings are not responsive to reason, do not attempt to settle disagreements when one or both of you is too emotional. Rather, choose a time when you are rational and willing to listen to each other. Until these conditions are met, table the discussion.

When you are emotionally and intellectually ready to deal with your conflicting values, be prepared to compromise, for that is the key to resolving your differences. This does not mean that one of you has to take a back seat to the other. Just bend a little instead of maintaining your self-righteousness.

Compromise requires you to *respect* your partner's feelings and views instead of ignoring them. It also requires you to ask appropriate questions that will lead you to a mutually acceptable solution. The following questions are steps in the right direction.

- "How do *you* propose we tackle the problem?"
- "If we follow your suggestions, what happens to *my* recommendations?"
- "OK, so you see it your way and I see it my way. How do you propose we reach an agreement so neither of us feels cheated?"

Such questions should not only help you understand your partner's frame of reference but also encourage her to think of workable solutions that are acceptable to you. Only by asking appropriate questions, similar to those suggested, can you determine alternatives your spouse might have in mind that you have not considered.

In addition to respecting your partner's views, you must insist that he respect yours. You can accomplish this objective by letting him know why you feel as you do and insisting that he listen to your proposal for a compromise. Such comments as "I believe I understand your feelings, but I want you to hear what I've got to say about it," or "Let me suggest how we can both get what we want," should set the stage for a productive interchange of ideas. Having established a climate of mutual respect, you will be more inclined to examine the pros and cons of your respective views and thereby reach some agreeable and satisfactory decision. Your decision may involve both of you giving a little, as in the following example:

SHE: I hate going to church every Sunday without you. Would it kill you to go with me, so I wouldn't feel strange when people ask me where you are?

HE: Can't you just say that I'm at home and leave it at that? You don't have to make excuses for me.

SHE: But going to church as a family is important.

HE: To you it is, but for me it would be a major sacrifice. Do you want me to make that kind of sacrifice?

SHE: Would you find it that offensive?

HE: Yes, I would.

SHE: Since I feel so strongly about going and you don't, how do you propose we resolve this problem?

HE: Would it help if I go, say, every other week?

SHE: That's a nice offer. But, as long as you feel so adamant about not going, each time you came with us you'd feel resentful.

HE: No, not really. I can handle it every other week. I'll agree to that. OK?

SHE: OK.

In this example, they also could have decided that it was not that important for him to go, if he considered it a major imposition. It could have been resolved with both agreeing to continue their respective practices rather than acceding to each other's wishes. Sometimes that is how differences are resolved. Each partner does what is right for him, without insisting that the other change.

Many of the examples in Chapter 1 concerned conflicts that stemmed from differences in values. It might be useful to go back and reexamine the approaches that were used in dealing with them constructively.

DIFFERENCES IN OPINIONS AND PERCEPTIONS

Couples also have differences of opinions and perceptions that are not based on values. Nevertheless, they create disagreements. Since these differences generally cannot be backed up with logic, one reasonable way of resolving them is to accept the fact that your spouse is entitled to a differing opinion. Like feelings, opinions are neither right nor wrong; they are just beliefs that we consider true. However, if you have reasons to believe that your spouse's opinion or perception is based on a false assumption, you have an obligation to make your position known, as in the following example.

HE: Why should I come with you to see your parents when they don't care whether I live or die? You're the only one they really care about.

SHE: I'm sorry you feel that way, because every time I talk with them they ask about you and are interested in what you're doing. In fact, last time I talked to them they wanted to know why you don't call them. Of course, they care about you.

HE: I didn't know that.

SHE: Well, it's true. Now will you come with me?

HE: I'll go this time and see for myself.

In this instance the woman might have disagreed with the

man's opinion in a destructive way by saying something like, "I'm sick and tired of constantly hearing about how rotten my parents are to you. You don't even have a decent thing to say about them." Had that been her response, the conflict would have evolved into a nasty and unnecessary argument.

STRATEGIES FOR RESOLVING DIFFERENCES

Regardless of the cause of your disagreements, you can resolve them more effectively by employing the strategies we'll discuss next. To begin with, you have to decide, based on what is said and how it is conveyed, who feels strongest about the issue being discussed. Good negotiating sense dictates that you give in on issues that are less important to you than to your spouse and hold your ground on matters that are extremely vital to you.

Admittedly, during the heat of conflict it is easy to forget all the suggestions and communication principles that have been presented thus far. Nevertheless, it is important that you try to be reasonable. If, for example, you sense that your spouse is introducing elements into your disagreements that are counterproductive or have nothing to do with the subject of your conflict, you must call her attention to what you see happening. A simple question such as, "What does that have to do with what we're discussing?" or a statement such as, "We seem to be fighting each other instead of looking for a solution," should get your discussion back on track. Don't allow yourself to be sidetracked by *reacting* to biting comments or implied criticisms that have nothing to do with the resolution of your conflict.

Suppose, for example, that you are arguing about any subject and your spouse says, "You're just like your mother." If you're not careful, you can get caught up in a senseless battle in which each partner tries to hurt the other more. By recognizing this as a sidetracking comment, however, you could respond, "We're not talking about my mother now; let's stick to the issue." In so doing, you avert a trap.

In another example, the question concerns whether or not to buy a certain item. Your spouse says, "If you hadn't spent the money on ___ , we would have no problems in buying ___ ." A constructive response would be, "You're probably right, but that's past. The question is whether we can *now* afford to buy ___ ." In this case, the criticism is acknowledged, and the sidetracking comment is averted by focusing on the current issue.

If the sidetracking comment your spouse directs toward you is truly painful, you might consider asking, "Are you trying to hurt me?" This question will force her to *think* about what she's doing or saying. Assuming she really doesn't want to hurt you, your question will cause her to develop a more productive tactic for dealing with the conflict.

While reaching a mutually satisfying solution is your primary aim in resolving your differences, do not *grudgingly* give in. All that does is breed resentment. Furthermore, if *you* sense your partner is giving in grudgingly, do not accept his concession on those terms. To do so would give him a weapon he can use against you in some future disagreement.

The type of conflicts we are discussing here are legitimate in that concrete problems need to be resolved. However, some conflicts are illegitimate because their purpose is to fulfill some negative prophecy that one or both partners have made about each other. Because such conflicts stem from deep feelings of hostility and bitterness, they invariably evolve into lose-lose battles. Accusations, false judgments, and attempts to *prove* the adversary wrong or thoughtless characterize these arguments. The result of these destructive battles is that both partners are left with emotional scars and bad feelings. Having fulfilled their negative prophecies and having "proven" what culprits their partners really are, they are worse off than they were before they began. What neither partner realizes is that in such battles nobody wins. Actually, both partners lose.

Regardless of the legitimacy of a conflict, the tendency to create and fall into traps that intensify problems and conflicts is ever present. The first step toward avoiding these traps is to recognize them; the second is to consider logical alternatives. These issues are considered in the next chapter.

3

Traps to Avoid in Dealing with Conflicts

As has been suggested earlier, some people are adept at employing diversionary tactics when dealing with conflicts. You will undoubtedly recognize some of these, since they are quite common. Because they serve no value, it makes sense to stop them.

Diversionary tactics are nothing more than smoke screens that obscure or camouflage the real problem. Furthermore, they direct one's energies away from developing a workable solution. Some of these methods include the following.

1. *Breast beating and complaining about how you are constantly being wronged.* This may gain some attention and perhaps make your spouse feel sorry for you. However, these emotional rewards do not last. After you have gotten your spouse's attention and sympathy, you are still faced with the problem. Worse yet, your spouse may rightfully feel that he is being manipulated by your emotional appeal.

2. *Putting your head in the sand, hoping the conflict will*

resolve itself. A problem does not go away just because you refuse to acknowledge its presence. That would amount to behaving like a child who covers his eyes and says, "You can't see me." Admitting a conflict exists is the first step toward resolving it.

3. *Running away from it by putting off facing the problem.* "I don't want to talk about it" is the typical reaction of people who are guilty of this tactic. They believe that by dodging their problem they can make it disappear. What actually happens is that the problem gets bigger and more unmanageable the longer you avoid discussing it.

4. *Blame-placing and attributing all your problems to others.* This last method is probably the most destructive tactic of all. Blame-placing, or projection, is an ego defense that takes the heat and responsibility off ourselves and places it on someone else's shoulders. To a large degree, projections are negative and false assumptions that are stated as accusations. The person employing this defense is *really* saying: "I don't want to take responsibility for my actions or decisions, so I'll make you the culprit." Here are some examples:

- "I would have suggested we do something together, but *you* probably would have said no."
- "I would have approached you, but *you* didn't seem interested."
- "*You* should have reminded me of my appointment."
- "If *you* had done your share, I would have done mine."
- "If it weren't for *you*, I could have been more successful."
- "I did it because I thought *you* wanted me to."
- "I didn't tell you because *you* wouldn't understand."

Why are these attempts at justifying your actions or inaction destructive? Because when you view your spouse as the cause of your failures, thoughtless mistakes, conflicts, or troubles, you disregard and therefore fail to examine *your own* contributions to the problem. That is, as long as you use your spouse as a scapegoat, you don't have to change. While it sounds like a simple approach to a problem—just place the blame on someone else—it does not work. The fact is that conflicts are created by two people, not one. Therefore, if each of you examines what you can do about the problem, a workable solution is possible.

It is easy to get caught up in the accusatory "It's not my fault; it's your fault" trap. And that is exactly what it is—a trap—because there is no graceful way of getting out of it. Making excuses and finding fault with your spouse breed nonproductive and sometimes destructive dialogues that do not bring you closer to a solution. So, how do you avoid such pitfalls?

Be forthright with yourself and your spouse. Making excuses to justify your reactions and placing blame on your spouse for not understanding you may appease you temporarily, but such accusations do not solve the problem. Problems and conflicts continue as long as ego defenses are employed. Therefore, admit to yourself and your partner the real reasons for your beliefs and actions. If your actions or reactions are based on certain fears, prejudices, or other emotional factors, state them. In short, by being forthright about your motives, you and your spouse will be better able to arrive at a compromise.

A couple I know disagreed on how to spend some extra cash they had. The wife wanted to invest it in stocks, while the husband wanted to put the money in a savings account. After considerable discussion, the husband revealed that his father had invested all his money in stocks and lost it. He also admitted a fear of losing his job and did not want to get caught without a substantial savings account he could rely on if his fears came to pass. Respecting his concerns, his wife suggested that they invest part of the money and place the rest in a savings account. This compromise, which was acceptable to him, would not have been reached had he withheld his fear. Had he taken the blame-placing route, he would have justified his fears by accusing his wife of imprudence in such matters.

Another couple I know had a conflict concerning an excellent job offer he received out of state. Because they had two children in high school, the wife felt that the gains he could make by accepting the position would not offset the problems this move might create for the children. He could not understand why she was adamant in her beliefs until she revealed her own anguish when her father moved the family while she was completing her junior year of high school. By being forced to go along with her father's decision, she felt that she missed out on graduating with her friends. She then told her husband that she never got over the feeling of being cheated and therefore would not want to subject their children to a similar trauma.

Reconsidering the job offer in light of this new information, they discussed the problem with the children. Convinced that no job was worth disrupting a family, the husband decided to continue in his current job while searching for a better one in the city where they were currently residing. Within several months he found a position that was comparable to the out-of-town offer.

As in the previous example, the man would not have been as agreeable to this decision had his wife failed to reveal the reasons for her resistance. Instead, he probably would have accused her of holding him back from advancing in his career—a false negative assumption. His wife, on the other hand, might have accused him of being insensitive to her wishes, which, without the information she shared, would have been a logical conclusion.

While defensiveness is common during arguments, telling your partner, "You're defensive," "You're making excuses," or "You're running away from the problem," only intensifies the argument. Realize that ego defenses are protections from emotional and intellectual pain. When your spouse is being defensive, regardless of what form it takes, she is protecting herself from certain realities, which she is unable to face. Telling her that she is making excuses, being unrealistic, finding fault with everyone but herself, too weak to face the truth, or lying to herself is disrobing her emotionally at a time when she may not be prepared to handle such candidness. All it can do is make her even more defensive and then offensive.

The alternative is to accept that defense. For example, say, "That may very well be true," and then direct the conversation toward a rational solution.

Let's examine two examples of how you can handle defensive reactions.

Dialogue 1

HE: If it weren't for you, I would have gone to graduate school.
SHE: You certainly had heavy responsibilities early in our marriage. But I'd back you if you wanted to start graduate school now.
HE: It's too late now.
SHE: Well, if you ever decide to do it, you know I'm behind you.

Notice that the wife allows her husband to hold on to his excuse (he probably could have gone to graduate school, as others have, if he had wanted to). At the same time, she leaves the door open for him to pursue further schooling if he chooses to. She could have said, "Don't blame me; other married people went to graduate school. You just didn't want to but used me as an excuse." Can you imagine the nasty argument that reaction would have produced?

Dialogue 2

SHE: If you hadn't insisted on having all those extras in the car, our payments wouldn't be as great as they are. Now we're paying for your mistakes and we're in trouble.
HE: Maybe I was unreasonable and I should have thought about the payments I was committing us to, but the question is, what can we do about the problem now?

In this example, the wife blames her inability to resist her husband's stubbornness and then attempts to make him feel guilty for his poor judgment. However, he accepts her defense and directs the conversation to what promises to be a reasonable solution. He could have responded with, "Well, if you hadn't agreed, I wouldn't have gotten all those extras." Where would that conversation have gone?

By accepting your spouse's defense you are not necessarily agreeing with him. You're just not arguing, since to do so would be futile and could create new conflicts.

Let's consider another diversionary tactic. This one is aimed at instigating a fight. But it is an unfair fight because, by its very nature, the person being baited cannot win. Consider the following example.

Dialogue 3

Sensing something is bothering his wife, who is slamming doors, pouting, and exhibiting other signs of anger, John asks: "What's wrong?" She replies, "If you don't know, I'm not going to tell you. Besides, if I have to tell you what's wrong, you wouldn't understand anyway."

In other words, if he had not asked, he would have been considered insensitive. By asking he is still obviously insensitive, since he has failed to recognize the problem on his own.

Here are three more examples of instances in which one person, for reasons that are not initially revealed, wants an argument and looks for ways to start one. The other person seems to be helpless and finds himself in a no-win situation.

Dialogue 4

SHE: When will you come home tonight?

HE: What's the matter, don't you trust me?

SHE: OK, forget it. Come home when you want.

HE: It makes no difference if I'm home or not, does it? (Which way does she turn? She's damned if she asks and damned if she doesn't ask.)

Dialogue 5

HE: Do you want to go out to dinner tonight?

SHE: Yes, I'd like that.

HE: I sure have a lot of work to get done before tomorrow's meeting.

SHE: Well, then, let's not go out tonight.

HE: But you're always complaining that we never go out. (If they go out, it's no good; but if they don't he can claim that she refused him.)

Dialogue 6

SHE: How do you like my hairdo?

HE: Gee, it looks real nice.

SHE: Then how come you didn't notice it until I asked you?

HE: I was preoccupied with something else. But it really does look nice.

SHE: No it doesn't; otherwise you would have said something before I called your attention to it. (This setup is an attempt to prove his thoughtlessness.)

As you can see, such no-win situations are designed to fulfill negative prophecies and therefore are unhealthy games. *Compatible* partners are not out to prove each other wrong or cruel, so don't make statements or ask leading questions that corner your spouse. What would you gain by it?

If *you* are the one who is being led into a no-win dilemma, expose the trap immediately. Statements such as these will make your spouse realize what he is doing:

- "It seems that, regardless of what I say or do, I'm wrong."
- "I sense a trap."
- "I get the feeling there is something else bothering you for you to corner me like this."

By exposing the trap early, you not only avoid a needless argument but also get your partner to talk about what is *really* bothering him.

Before proceeding to Part II, it would be worthwhile to read the next two dialogues. In both of them, the statements of each person are analyzed in italics following the statement. The first dialogue takes place between an engaged couple who are college seniors. While they are not married, their conversation is a good one to study because it clearly illustrates both the violation and effective use of several important communication principles.

HE: Do you want to go to the basketball game tonight?

SHE: I guess so. *Her unenthusiastic response suggests a potential problem. He should have responded to it by saying something like, "Sounds like you're not too excited about going." However, he says nothing.*

(Later)

SHE: Where are Debbie and Harry going tonight?

HE: They're going to some kind of play and dinner.

SHE: It must be nice. It seems like they're always going to nice places. *This is an implied negative criticism. Rather than being straightforward and telling him that she would like to do that sometime, she hints at it. But the hint is at the same time an attack on how this couple spends their time. An appropriate response would be, "Are you saying we don't?"*

HE: Yep, I guess so. Would you like to do that sometime? *While he picked up her implications by suggesting that he would also like to do that, he failed to acknowledge her emotions. However, he did not become defensive or angry with her. Rather, he chose to hear what she said and responded to her words.*

SHE: I won't hold my breath. Anyway, I don't really care; basketball games are OK. *Here is where the real trouble begins. Rather than responding to his question by telling him that she would indeed enjoy that, she attacks him further, saying in effect that she doesn't consider his question and implied invitation sincere. As you can see, she has made a negative assumption that he is not interested in taking her to nice places and has set up a negative prophecy that he'll never follow through on the invitation. Now she must follow through and fulfill that prophecy herself. She starts in that direction by lying to him, "Basketball games are OK."*

(*Later*)

HE: Friday the Bulls are on the road, so I figured we could go to my brother's basketball game on Saturday. *He ignored her implied accusations and took her statement about basketball being OK at face value. By failing to respond to the emotional part of her statement ("I won't hold my breath"), he is falling into a trap. He might have asked her what she meant by her comment, e.g., "What do you mean you won't hold your breath?" rather than disregard it.*

SHE: Don't bother to ask. I can't stand that when you take it for granted that I'm going out with you just because it's Saturday night. *She has a point, but her anger has nothing to do with his not asking. She is bothered by other things but isn't sharing her feelings with him openly. However, his lack of sensitivity is intensifying her anger.*

HE: OK. I'm sorry. Do you want to go? *Rather than asking her what is* really *bothering her, he again takes her statement at face value and responds to it.*

SHE: I guess so. I wouldn't want to miss a basketball game. God forbid! *Her concession clearly suggests that she is getting ready for a martyr role. Furthermore, her dishonesty continues, as do her implied accusations and digs.*

HE: What are you getting so mad about? *The light finally dawns, so he does the only reasonable thing he could; he asks for an explanation of her emotional reaction.*

SHE: I'm not mad. It's just that we never do anything else. *She is finally leveling with him, after her initial lie about not being mad.*

HE: Don't say never. We went to a party last week. *Again he failed to read between the lines. Instead, he takes a defensive posture. This is one place where it would have been appropriate to ask, "Never?"*

SHE: Oh, I forgot, and who was the winner of the game you ended up watching? And now that you brought it up, we did go to a football game a couple of weeks ago, a tennis tournament Tuesday, and a baseball meeting last Friday. *Now we have it. She is upset about his narrow interests. But notice that she has been saving up her anger. Worse than that, she is still not telling him directly how she feels about their limited social life. She also isn't telling him why this narrow interest bothers her.*

HE: Well, then what are you complaining about? *He doesn't get her point. His lack of sensitivity is showing. At the same time, however, she is asking him to play guessing games.*

SHE: Nothing. I'm kind of tired, I guess. *She continues to lie and to deny her anger.*

HE: We don't have to go to the basketball game if you don't want to.

SHE: No, that's OK. I'll go. *Although he finally gets her message, she must play out her martyr role so she can hold it against him later. To accept his offer would sabotage her plans.*

(*Later*)

HE: Joe was telling me about that new lounge that opened up. He says it's real nice and we ought to go there some time. *He's still trying.*

SHE: I heard it was nice. *Is she waiting for another invitation?*

HE: What's wrong? You're not saying much.

SHE: I'm sick of hearing where everyone else has been, where everyone else goes; I don't want to hear it. *She is apparently assuming that he is teasing her with the information he relayed. She was so intent on hearing what she wanted to hear that the last part of his statement fell on deaf ears. Had she listened and responded to his entire message, she would have said, "Yes, we ought to go there sometime."*

HE: I thought you liked nice places.

SHE: Well, considering we never go anyplace besides sports activities, I don't have too much to say about anything else. *She insists on hitting him over the head with a two-by-four and maintaining her martyr role. Furthermore, she is not budging one inch to help him—or herself—resolve her concerns.*

HE: Well, you could suggest something else. *He tries to maintain the discussion on a rational level and to keep the dialogue from straying away from the subject at hand.*

SHE: Why should I? You probably wouldn't go anyway. *We finally have the prophecy stated clearly. Do you notice the projection? Here she is justifying her failure to initiate suggestions by assuming that* he *would not be responsive.*

HE: How do you know unless you ask?

SHE: Because I know—sports, sports, sports, that's all that matters to you.

HE: How about next week instead of going to the game we'll go to a nice dinner and show or something? *He continues not to defend his position. Rather, he suggests doing something that would truly be of interest to her.*

SHE: Oh, I bet you'll have fun. If it isn't sports, it's not worth it. You'll be bored. So just forget it. *She is not about to let him ruin her prophecy. She wants to believe that he doesn't care about her, and she will not allow anything he says to dissuade her from this false assumption. So she uses another projection—"You'll be bored,"—to fulfill her martyr role.*

HE: Do you still want to go to the game next week? *His insensitivity is showing again.*

SHE: What difference does it make if I go or not? It's the game that's important; that's what matters, not me. Besides, I think I just might go out, dress up, and have a good time for a change. *The self-fulfilling prophecy is fulfilled.*

Note that he might have, very early in the dialogue, told her what he suspected. Specifically, he could have said, "I get the feeling that no matter what I suggest or say to you, you're going to believe what you want. Is that true or can we decide to do something that you would enjoy?" Such a statement would cut off this nonsensical game at an early point. Furthermore, it would force her to be honest with herself as well as with him.

The next dialogue is an argument I recently overheard in a restaurant.

HE (looking at the menu): This food sure looks rich in calories. There must be at least a thousand calories in the chicken special alone, not to mention the dessert.

SHE: I think I can handle it. Calories don't bother me. I just want to enjoy my food.

HE: Yes, but by the end of the evening you can turn into a balloon if you're not careful. *His use of the word* you *is unfortunate. In fact, this entire statement was unnecessary. He could have simply replied, "You're fortunate that you don't worry about calories like I do." Or he could have changed the subject, talked about his own concerns about gaining weight, or said nothing.*

SHE: Are you trying to tell me I'm fat? *He didn't say that. But her insistence on taking his comment personally resulted in this reaction. She could have just as easily let his comment pass, or she could have said, "I suppose one can, if he is not careful."*

HE: No, I'm just pointing out to you that we should be more calorie-conscious. *At this point again she could have said, "I suppose," and then dropped it. After all, the man is expressing an opinion, to which he is entitled. But, as before, she interprets this opinion as a personal affront.*

SHE: Oh, I see. You're trying to tell me that I overeat. Why don't you just come out and say it instead of beating around the bush? *She's not about to let him off the hook. He got himself into a jam with his nonthinking small talk, and, because of her particular sensitivities, she's making all kinds of unwarranted and false assumptions.*

HE: I am not trying to make fun of your weight, but—

SHE (interrupting): But what? I better start keeping a calorie count, right?

HE: Quite the contrary. But if you want to feel this way, you can. *Now he really does it. Obviously, he doesn't know when to keep his mouth shut, when to stop talking. An apology would have been in order after her last comment. All he had to say was, "Hey, I'm sorry this has gotten out of hand. I was just making a general statement; it really had nothing to do with you. Let's just enjoy our dinner."*

SHE: Well, I've got news for you. You're not perfect either. You drive like a maniac, you were late for our date, and on top of all that you brought me to this raunchy restaurant. I don't know why I ever agreed to go out with you. *This is a clear case of sidetracking. Now it's a question of what she can say to hurt him. After all, one good hurt deserves another.*

HE (raising his voice to compete with hers): Don't you think you're doing me a favor by going out with me. I could have asked a more mature girl to go out with me instead of you. *He's not about to take her insults lying down.*

SHE: Take me home. Don't bother talking to me anymore.

They got up and left before ordering.

Ridiculous as this dialogue is, in essence it is similar to many we have all heard. It illustrates how people can blow out of proportion a comment that may be perfectly innocent. It also illustrates the difficulties many people have in apologizing when they are inadvertently insensitive. Her sensitivity to her weight, and his failure to apologize or explain his comment following her initial response ruined the evening for both.

PART II

The True Meaning of Love

4

The Power of Love

L ove brought you together, and love will keep you together.
That is the power of love. But what is the nature of this
power, which has been the subject of so many thousands of songs,
books, and poems?

Emotions that attract two people to each other are unquestionably the main source of this power. However, that power must be
nourished with loving attitudes and actions if it is to maintain its
vitality and endure. It is people's failure to provide such nour-
ishment that weakens and even destroys the emotional bond that
first drew them together. In this chapter we will talk about how
you can strengthen your emotional love rather than allow it to
falter.

Perched in the center of the family room mantel in my home is
my basic philosophy for establishing and maintaining those relationships I value. These words, which I wrote and had framed as a
gift for my wife, serve as a constant reminder of my commitments
to the special people in my life—my immediate family and my

good friends. They also serve as a constant reminder of my standards for gauging the depth and quality of any new relationships I form.

**LOVE =
MUTUAL
RESPECT
AND
TRUST**

**Spiced with those special feelings
that draw two people together.**

Love in this equation means caring in the broadest sense. Love may exist between any two people, be they parent and child, husband and wife, siblings, or friends. The feelings and the basis of the attraction in each of these relationships are different. Nevertheless, if *genuine* love exists between two people, their actions and attitudes are aimed at bringing out the best in each other. Whether their love is fraternal, filial, or romantic, their primary concern is the other person, the object of their love, rather than their own selfish interests and desires.

If all this is true, how can people be unkind, inconsiderate, and even cruel toward persons they supposedly love? My only explanation is that they have a distorted notion of love. The fact is that you cannot *genuinely* love someone and at the same time be cruel, unkind, or thoughtless toward that person.

A caring relationship, whereby two people create an environment that brings out the best in each other, must be based on mutual respect and trust, as well as emotional love. But each relationship is unique in the special feelings that add spice to it. The depth and quality of feelings you have varies widely for your spouse, children, parents, and friends. Yet you love all of them. While neither you nor I can describe each of those feelings, we can describe actions and attitudes that demonstrate respect and trust.

THE MEANING OF RESPECT

No one likes being ignored. No one likes to have his feelings, opinions, or desires disregarded. Yet, these are common occurrences in marriages, as well as in other important relationships. These occurrences are probably the greatest cause of marital difficulties. Why? Because all of us need to feel worthy and important in the eyes of our loved ones. We need to feel that they care about what we think, feel, and desire. These needs are fulfilled by actions and attitudes that demonstrate respect.

Because respect is a key requirement for building any close and cooperative relationship, let us examine the concept more closely. The word literally means to look at *(spect)* again *(re)*. When you respect someone, you give that person a second and third look or thought, as opposed to ignoring the individual. You seriously consider, rather than disregard, that person's feelings, actions, abilities, knowledge, and ideas. Being sensitive to those things that are important to the people you associate with, especially people who are important to you, and expressing your sensitivity in ways that show you care is the essence of a respectful attitude. Stated differently, a respectful attitude affirms other people's human worth. The attitude says, in effect, "You are important as a person and deserve to be acknowledged and treated as such." It does not imply agreements, however. You can be considerate, i.e., respectful toward others, but still not agree with or approve of what they say or do.

Obviously, it would be impractical to give second thoughts to everyone you meet or know. If you did, you would accomplish little for yourself. But, because your spouse is not just another person, you cannot afford to turn your back on her. You cannot afford to be insensitive to those things that are important to your spouse.

A respectful attitude toward your marriage partner recognizes important needs all of us have, regardless of our position, occupation, status, and sex. We all need to feel accepted for who we are; we need to feel that our opinions matter; we need to feel that others care about our feelings and beliefs; we need recognition for our efforts. Realizing that your spouse's feelings are as important to him as yours are to you is the first step toward fulfilling this vital need.

In general, all you really have to do is to acknowledge the significance of your spouse's perceptions and emotions. Specifically, the following eight actions and attitudes will demonstrate your respect for your marriage partner:

1. Give your spouse as much consideration as you would any stranger you might want to impress.

"You are nicer and more considerate to strangers than you are to me." This fairly common complaint points to the fact that many couples take each other for granted, believing that their partners will be available and responsive to them *regardless* of their actions. With strangers, however, particularly those they want to impress, they know that there are no second chances. Not wanting to risk losing out on whatever they want from these persons, they are cordial, respectful, and willing to extend themselves to achieve their objectives. But they do not think such actions are necessary with their spouses, since they perceive no risk of losing them.

Unfortunately, that risk is ever present, as one of my clients discovered. Despite the fact that Marla had asked her husband, Frank, to discuss some major concerns she had about their ten-year marriage, he ignored her. According to Marla, Frank told her that it was no big deal and that she was making a mountain out of a molehill. He apparently could not find time to talk to Marla about her concerns. Yet, Frank expected her to be attentive to his needs, despite his failure to consider hers. When I suggested to Marla that Frank come to see me so we could work out their problems, his response to her was, "It's not my problem; it's yours." Frank's failure to respect her desires, and his taking her for granted, resulted in a divorce.

Immediately after Marla's divorce petition was served on Frank, he made an appointment to see me. During the hour he repeatedly said, "What a fool I've been. If I had only listened to her rather than ignore her, this wouldn't have happened. It's my fault for taking her for granted. I sure learned my lesson."

Failing to realize that the emotional bond that draws them together is not indestructible, couples who take each other for granted can easily engender an attitude that says, "What difference does it make what I do? You don't care or appreciate it anyway." The offended spouse, in self-defense, may seek retribution for the hurt he is suffering. Once it gets to that stage, problems multiply.

To avoid such problems you must adopt the attitude that your marriage partner is an important and valuable person in your life whose friendship you have to cultivate. Realize that your spouse is also a valuable source of information who can help you understand her private world. All that is required of you is to listen.

While taking your spouse for granted may be a natural habit, you can be sure it will destroy your relationship. On the other hand, thanking him for something he did, saying "please" when you make requests, complimenting her for a job well done, asking how things are getting along, offering your help on any problems he has, cordially greeting her when you see each other after being apart, and making time available for him may seem like insignificant gestures, but they mean a great deal to your spouse. Isn't this the kind of treatment you would prefer?

2. Express delight in your partner's achievements and show appreciation for his efforts.

When you do something you consider an accomplishment, don't you want to be recognized for it? Of course, as do most people. But when that recognition comes from people you care about or hold in esteem, it really makes you feel good. For this reason it is vital that you commend your spouse on his achievements, as well as on his efforts. Whether or not *you* consider his efforts or achievements significant is immaterial. If he is pleased with what he's done, it behooves you to share in his joy and compliment him for his achievement. To do so shows respect for the things he does that are meaningful to him.

Comments such as those on the next page will encourage your spouse to continue doing those things that warrant similar compliments. Equally important, they tell him that you consider the results of his labors worthy of your approval.

- "Gee, that's great."
- "I'm really proud of you."
- "That sure was nice the way you handled the problem."
- "I'm really happy for you."
- "I appreciate what you did."

Under no circumstances should you put down your spouse's accomplishments or efforts.

3. Be flexible when making decisions that affect your spouse.

Major decisions concerning such matters as career changes, moves to another city, or costly purchases involve both you and your spouse and therefore must be made jointly. The decision you arrive at must be the best one for the relationship. You cannot assume the position that what you want is the only thing that matters. That attitude discounts your partner's thoughts and feelings.

Prior to settling on a decision, each alternative should be discussed thoroughly in terms of what would be gained and lost if it were adopted. Remember, your individual desires should be respected, but you are also a member of a partnership. In this dual role, it is essential that you consider major decisions from both perspectives.

4. Allow your partner time to be alone. Also encourage your spouse to spend some leisure time with other friends.

Vital as it is for couples to spend time together, it is equally important that each partner has time alone—to collect her thoughts and relax fully so she can recharge her emotions. Being in the presence of another person, even with someone you love, can be draining and can also limit the freedom that being alone offers. By respecting your partner's need for solitude, even if it is only for 15 minutes or half an hour, you are contributing to his well-being.

While doing things together, just like being together, is vital to the health of your relationship, both partners need stimulation from others. Encouraging your spouse to seek out people with whom he can share interests that you may not appreciate or enjoy demonstrates your respect for his individuality. At the same time, you too will benefit. When your spouse shares his social and intellectual experiences with you, you will learn and grow along with him. Both of your individual experiences will give you new and different things to talk about.

5. Do not ask your spouse to do anything she considers offensive.

Everyone has a right to her own likes and dislikes. Marriage does not obligate you or your spouse to abdicate that right. Therefore, insisting that your partner perform acts he considers highly offensive would strain the relationship. It is tantamount to saying, "If *I* don't consider it offensive to do what I'm asking of you, neither should you," or "What pleases me should also please you," or "Your likes should be the same as my likes." The underlying message in all these inferred statements is that your partner does not matter, as long as your desires are satisfied.

In defense of your point of view, you might say, "Yes, but if my spouse loves me wouldn't he do what I ask, regardless of whether or not it is offensive?" My response would be, "If you loved your partner, would you insist he make the major sacrifice you are requesting?" Of course not—not if you cherish the friendship.

6. Solicit opinions, ideas, and help from your spouse on important problems or issues.

You and your partner are *not* equal; you are different. Aside from your sexual differences, you probably do not possess the same abilities or personal qualities. If you feed on each other's strengths and offset one another's weaknesses, your differences can be vital to the personal growth of both of you and can also intensify your relationship.

One major advantage of forming any partnership is that it unifies people with similar values and complementary skills in their pursuit of common interests and goals. People in business establish such relationships because they anticipate having richer lives together than they could have alone. By viewing each other as vital resources and respecting each other's knowledge and skills, they can attain their anticipated goals.

Assuming you and your partner complement each other, consult her on her areas of expertise and solicit her opinions when appropriate. Being asked for our opinions and help on important matters is the most direct way of being told we are respected. However, when you make such requests, make it clear that you are not necessarily asking him to make decisions for you or to tell you what you "should" do. Tell your spouse that you only want his point of view or ideas, which you value and will consider seriously. This will minimize the chance of your spouse becoming offended if you choose a course of action that is different from the one he or she would have taken.

Two conditions should be observed when you solicit opinions from your partner. First, when they are offered, don't undermine them, however outrageous they may seem. Acknowledge them with such statements as, "I appreciate your opinion" or "That's interesting; let me think about it." The fact is, opinions are neither right nor wrong. They represent a person's perceptions, to which he is entitled. Even though you may not see it the same way, if you make the mistake of pooh-poohing his opinions, you may unwittingly be shutting the door to further communications. Don't forget, when your spouse voices his opinions, he truly believes he is right. Undermining these beliefs are attacks on his ego; that is no way to foster a give-and-take relationship.

Second, don't ask for opinions if your mind is already made up. Aside from being insulting, it invites needless arguments when the opinions you receive do not agree with your decisions. The time to ask for opinions is when you are open to fresh viewpoints, not when you want a rubber-stamp approval. Under such conditions it is more forthright to state the decision you have reached and then request your spouse's support.

7. Realize that your spouse's emotional response to people and events is part of his uniqueness that must be respected.

When you married, you had no choice but to inherit your partner's family—your in-laws. Admittedly, you can't be expected to have the same feelings toward them as your spouse does. But for your partner's sake and in the name of respect, you would be wise to appreciate the importance these relationships have for him. Furthermore, consider the obligations your partner has toward his family and support your spouse in doing whatever he feels is necessary to avoid alienating them. The risks of undermining your partner's emotional attachments to his family, just because you may not like them, far outweighs the value you could gain by going along with what has to be done to preserve domestic tranquility.

Similarly, if your spouse has personal friends whose company you do not enjoy, let her know how you feel about them. At the same time, tell your partner that you would not discourage her from seeing them, if that is what she wants.

8. Make undivided time available to discuss feelings or concerns that are upsetting your partner—and listen.

Your partner's disposition undoubtedly has a profound affect on you. When your spouse is in good spirits you probably feel uplifted and have a desire to share in her joys. But when your partner is in physical or emotional pain, her state may add to your burdens and limit your effectiveness. Since you have a great deal to gain by being available to your spouse for important discussions, and much to lose if you put her off, consider the time you give to your partner, when she asks for it, as an investment in your happiness.

If for some reason your spouse does not ask to talk with you, even though he is upset, don't stand on ceremony. Go to him. Simply say something like, "Looks like you're bothered by something. Do you want to talk about it?" If he says no, just tell him you are available whenever he's ready to discuss the problem.

In summary, you respect your spouse when you convey, through your actions and words, that she is an important person in your life whose opinions, feelings, and desires matter a great deal to you. By being respectful toward your partner, you increase your chances of gaining his or her respect.

HOW TO COMMAND RESPECT

Vital as it is to respect your spouse, you must also command respect from him. Notice the use of *command* versus *demand*. To command your spouse's respect you first must believe that you are worthy of decent treatment. Once that belief is instilled in you, you will develop your own standards of how you want to be treated. Having these standards, you must insist that others, including your spouse, respect them. If you are strong in your resolve that you will not tolerate less than decent treatment, you will no longer be viewed as a pushover who can be manipulated. Rather, you will receive the respect you deserve.

These standards serve as a defense against the human tendency to take advantage of anyone who allows it. They are a defense against the quality—which all of us have to different degrees—to try to get away with whatever we can.

Your partner's violation of any of the eight principles for demonstrating respect threatens your belief that you are worthy of decent treatment. Violations of the communication principles we discussed earlier also threaten your self-respect. Don't, under any circumstances, ignore these threats, but stick to the standards you have set for yourself.

The first time you feel that your self-respect is threatened—i.e., you are ignored or given less consideration than you believe you deserve—let your partner know that you will not tolerate her disrespect. Let her know as soon as possible that you are entitled to the same consideration she expects from you. If words don't convey your message, you may have to employ other tactics to gain your partner's attention.

Two examples come to mind that show how attention can be gained when you are not getting the respect you deserve.

The first involves Sharon, who is an excellent cook but never received compliments from her husband or any other member of her family on the meals she prepared. Even when she prepared their favorite meals, they took her efforts for granted. Sometimes she would ask, "Did you enjoy it?" And, of course, they would all indicate in their own ways that they had. But they never volunteered these reactions.

One evening, in anger, she simply placed some bread, an unopened can of tuna, and a can opener on the table. When the family members inquired about this unappealing meal, she replied, "Apparently it makes no difference to you what I make for dinner, since you never compliment me unless I ask for it. So I thought you didn't really care what you ate." They got the message, and they did not take her labors for granted again.

Another example: Joanne regularly made social plans without consulting her husband. While Bart pleaded with her to discuss these matters with him before making arrangements, she persisted in ignoring his requests. One evening he just refused to attend a dinner party that she had scheduled without consulting him. Being too embarrassed to go by herself, she canceled the engagement, claiming a sudden illness. As drastic as Bart's tactics were for commanding respect, they worked.

Quiet strength is a phrase that accurately describes people who command respect. That phrase suggests that the respect they receive does not come from pounding fists on tables, yelling, or *demanding* the kind of treatment they deserve. They also don't have to remind others too often of their human worth. Their strength comes from not allowing others to use, abuse, or misuse them.

You too can command respect from your spouse by believing you deserve it and upholding your standards. On the other hand, if you permit your spouse to get away with actions that violate your standards and take advantage of your good nature, you will invite more of the same behavior. That behavior becomes increasingly more difficult to control the longer it is tolerated.

HOW TO DEMONSTRATE YOUR TRUSTWORTHINESS

Marriage partners need to depend on and confide in each other. They need to share feelings and thoughts that cannot be shared with anyone else. Without mutual trust these needs cannot be fulfilled.

When mutual trust exists between couples, each partner believes that his spouse's actions and motives are honorable.

Thus, they are more likely to accept each other's criticisms, opinions, directions, ideas, reasons for doing or not doing something, and any other statements or actions that could be viewed either positively or negatively. On the other hand, misinterpretations, paranoid thinking, secretiveness, lack of mutual confidence, and fear exist between couples who distrust each other.

The extent to which your spouse can and will trust you depends on your own trustworthiness. Being human, and therefore imperfect, none of us is totally trustworthy. Nevertheless, you can take steps toward achieving this ideal objective by adhering to the following seven guides.

1. Do not say or do anything to deliberately hurt your spouse.

People we love have the power to hurt us deeply if they so desire. Having entrusted you with this power, by virtue of her love, your partner needs to believe that you would not misuse that power by saying or doing things that you know will hurt her deeply. You know, for example, that it would be emotionally painful to her if you were to criticize her in public or say and do other things that would embarrass her. Knowing your spouse as you do, you are aware of all of her weak spots. To take advantage of these weaknesses would undermine her trust in you. There is no room for spite in a good marriage or, for that matter, in any valued interdependent relationship.

You may sometimes unintentionally hurt your spouse with a statement or an action. When that happens, and you realize afterward what you've done, apologize immediately. Attempt to convince him that your thoughtlessness was not deliberate. Hopefully, your sincerity will minimize the hurt.

2. Do not use anything your spouse has said or done as a destructive weapon. Never betray a confidence.

Fear, uncertainty, and suspicion are the enemies of trust and are barriers to honest communication. The question that goes through most people's minds before sharing their thoughts, feelings, or other personal information is, "If I tell him _____, how will he react?" If your spouse is afraid of what you will say or do when she tells you something, particularly if it's something you may not approve of, it may be that she does not trust you to be understanding, accepting, or open-minded. Lacking this trust, she will decide that it is safer to keep these vital thoughts and feelings to herself.

I'm not suggesting that these fears are unnatural. On the contrary, they are quite natural. All of us have been disappointed by people who, after we've shared a part of ourselves, criticized us unmercifully, "rained on our parade," or violated our confidence. Most of us have also been the source, as well as the victim, of such behavior. Being aware of these human frailties, it is understandable that we are reluctant to share vital information and feelings with others.

But the relationship marriage partners have with each other is special, and they have to do everything possible to dispel or allay the fears their spouses may harbor.

To convince your spouse that it is safe to disrobe emotionally and intellectually before you and that you are not amassing a "file" of misdeeds that might be hurled at him some day, *don't judge him*. Don't put down the things he tells you. Respond to them as you would to any emotions. Treat the secrets he shares with you as privileged information that cannot be divulged to *anyone*. In short, don't hurt him with the information he shares with you.

If you are bothered about something your spouse said, inform her of your feelings and the reasons for your reaction. You can do that without insulting her and causing her to regret ever telling you anything.

One couple I was seeing was plagued by problems that revolved around this very issue. Marge complained that her husband didn't tell her anything of importance and that their discussions were generally quite superficial. When we delved into her complaint, Nick finally told her that in the past, whenever he shared a problem that he had with a supervisor or fellow worker, she reminded him that he had had similar difficulties in previous jobs. Then she related specific incidents to make her point.

When Marge admitted to having done that, Nick said, "You know, Marge, rather than helping me with the problem I was having, you knocked me down with all that other stuff I told you about. Those stories I told you just boomeranged. So I decided to stop telling you anything.''

3. Do not cause your spouse to regret or feel guilty for bringing up a problem that involves you.

Suppose you said or did something that bothered your spouse. Would you want him to tell you about it? If you would, you must be willing to accept his comments as valid and constructive criticisms. Since his criticisms regarding your conduct can be useful guides for future action, discouraging him from leveling with you would not serve your best interests. Discouraging honesty and forthrightness is not always obvious, as is evident in the following dialogue.

HE: You look like something's bothering you.

SHE: It'll pass.

HE: Well, what is it?

SHE: Since I've been working, I not only have my job to worry about, but also the house. You haven't offered once to help me. It's not just my house, you know. I wish you'd realize it and give me a hand.

HE: Who asked you to work? It was your idea.

SHE: You asked me what was bothering me, so I told you. What good did it do?

HE: So quit your job.

SHE: Just forget I said anything.

He may indeed forget she said anything, but you can be sure that she will think several times before confronting him with a concern that involves him. How can she when he makes her feel guilty for working, something she wants to do? While she may continue performing both jobs, his reactions will cause her to harbor ill feelings that can grow out of proportion.

Remember, your partner's criticisms or descriptions of problems that involve you are invitations to resolve them and to improve your relationship. If you can't be trusted to be responsive to your partner's concerns, don't expect cooperation from him when *you* need *him*.

4. Be truthful and open about things that matter to both of you. Don't build an invisible wall between you.

This principle is a corollary to the preceding one. If you are bothered by something your partner has or has not said or done, tell her. Do not hold it in or pout about it. Isn't it possible that she may not be aware of her offense? Only by telling her can you be sure that she knows how you feel and what she did to cause the feeling.

Harboring bad feelings and building invisible walls is a lose-lose situation. You can't possibly resolve the problem, since she is not aware of its existence, and she remains in the doghouse without knowing why. In the end, neither of you gain anything. On the other hand, if you let her know what is bothering you, you have at least gotten your problem off your chest, and there is a chance of working it out to your satisfaction.

In other words, your spouse can trust you if he is certain that you are not keeping things from him that could, at some future time, escalate into a cold war. An example of this occurred when one of my clients came to me, along with his wife, because he wanted a divorce. When I asked him my usual question—"What is it that you want from your wife that she hasn't been fulfilling?"—he replied, "Nothing. She's given me everything I need." Believing he wasn't being truthful, I asked his wife if I could have a few minutes alone with him. When I posed the same question after she had left, he listed all the things he disliked about her. "Did you ever tell her?" I asked. "No," he replied. "I didn't want to hurt her feelings." The marriage ended in divorce. Cause of death: husband killing wife with kindness.

5. Be available emotionally, if not physically, when your spouse needs you.

An unalterable fact of life is that each individual experiences his own pains, burdens, anxieties, and ecstacies in a unique way. When you ache, feel inner turmoil, or receive special recognition for something you have done, the feelings you experience are yours and yours alone. Nobody else can possibly feel the sensations you feel. Yet, during these difficult or joyous times you need to know that there is at least one person you can trust to be at your side, hold your hand, and give you emotional support. Being married, you would like that someone to be your spouse.

Having you to lean on or to share joys is important to your partner, since this tells your spouse that you care and are deeply involved in whatever he or she is experiencing. If you cannot depend on each other for comfort, encouragement, and support, who can you turn to? The alternatives available would undoubtedly weaken the emotional bond between you.

6. Follow through on your promise to fulfill your partner's requests, as well as your own objectives.

When you keep your promises to your spouse, you establish your credibility and dependability, both of which affirm your trustworthiness.

Both you and your partner are accustomed to dealing with people who make empty promises, whose actions belie their words, and who are too preoccupied with themselves to think about your desires. For these reasons marriage partners need to feel that their happiness is one of their spouses' prime concerns. By following through on the promises or commitments you make to your spouse, you are saying, "I am thinking of you, even when you are not with me," or "I care enough about you to do those things that make you happy," or "I am not like most of the other people you deal with; you can believe what I say."

Marriage partners also need to feel that their spouses are capable of maintaining control of their own lives by fulfilling those obligations to themselves that they have assumed. Spouses need assurance that their partners are mature and responsible people who are not totally dependent on them. That assurance exists when you exercise sound judgments and make prudent decisions that enable you to achieve the goals and objectives you set for yourself.

7. Be consistent in demonstrating your respect and dependability.

In the final analysis, consistency is the key to establishing your trustworthiness. By consistently being respectful toward your spouse and by consistently demonstrating that you can be trusted, you reduce communication barriers. While few things in life are predictable, it is comforting to know that you can at least feel secure in your belief that your spouse is a true friend who will always come through for you in ways that nobody else can.

Part III

Personalizing Your Marriage Partnership

5

Getting to Know Your Partner

N ow that you have read and studied the principles for communicating effectively, you are ready to consider and discuss what you and your spouse have to offer each other; your responsibilities to each other; your mutual expectations, needs, and desires; and how you will honor the agreements you reach. In effect, you will be writing your own personal marriage vows, which will make your relationship unique and right for you. All of this information will be developed through a series of carefully designed exercises. While some general guidelines on your responsibilities as marriage partners are included, only you can work out the details.

You are cautioned not to rush and begin a new exercise until you have fully discussed the one you are working on. This is not a crash course that must be completed in a specific number of days. It is an ongoing learning program that must be approached with the same perseverance, determination, and patience you would employ if you were to embark on a self-improvement course that offers long-range benefits. To gain maximum value, you must work at the course slowly, deliberately, and regularly. If you set aside two to four hours a week of uninterrupted time, you will gain what you hoped for when you purchased this book.

Let us begin with some basic views on marriage. Remember that these are my personal views and should be considered only as loose guidelines. You may wish to discuss these with your spouse before you begin the exercises that follow.

WHAT MAKES MARRIAGE A SPECIAL PARTNERSHIP

Throughout this book I have referred to marriage as a partnership because that is what I believe it should be. If it is to be a healthy, growing partnership, your physical attraction toward each other should be supported by a foundation consisting of the following ideals.

1. Marriage is a merger of two people, possessing unique personalities and abilities, whose aims are to achieve more from life together than each could attain alone. Why else form a partnership?

2. Marriage is a 100-100 relationship, with both individuals giving as much of themselves as they are capable of giving. Through such unselfish giving, both partners help each other grow as people. The notion that marriage is a 50-50 relationship, or some other percentage that is less than 100-100, is a myth. It suggests that each partner is not giving all that he or she is capable of giving to the relationship.

3. Marriage is a complementary relationship, with both partners feeding on each other's strengths while offsetting one another's weaknesses. You certainly wouldn't want to be married to someone who had identical strengths and weaknesses to yours, since such a relationship could only stunt your growth.

This would be an opportune time to discuss these ideals with your partner. Do you both agree on them? How do your feelings differ?

In contrast, a healthy partnership should *not* be:

1. *An employer-employee relationship.* This is a marketing relationship, which implies that one person must be subordinate to the other. While this arrangement works in business, a spouse who is treated as a hired hand will most likely resent it.

2. *A parent-child relationship.* Parents generally set rules for children to follow. Being in charge of the home environment, parents typically have the last word on what is done and when. Furthermore, children are often shielded from the concerns and responsibilities that parents have.

A spouse who is treated as a child feels relatively unimportant and believes he is more of a burden than a partner. The partner who assumes a parentlike role is likely to tire from it and therefore feel justified in seeking more satisfying relationships outside the home.

3. *A possessive relationship.* A spouse is not an acquisition. To view her as such assumes that by virtue of marriage one person owns the other. The fact is that *things* are owned, but people should not be. People who view their spouses as possessions tend to treat them and talk about them as objects that serve certain prescribed functions. This is similar to a marketing relationship and, as such, deteriorates when their respective functions are no longer required.

4. *A competitive relationship.* When two people compete, there has to be a winner and a loser. In a true partnership both partners win; there need not be a loser.

HOW YOU PERCEIVE YOUR SPOUSE

As you know, we do not perceive ourselves as others do. You may, for example, view yourself as reasonable and flexible when you may, in fact, be unreasonable and inflexible in many situations. Similarly, your spouse may perceive one of your qualities as a strength, while you have never thought of it as such, or he may view a particular quality as a weakness, while you believe it to be a strength.

By knowing which of your qualities your partner considers strengths and which weaknesses, you will be better able to understand his favorable as well as unfavorable reactions to you. After completing Exercises 1 and 2, you will each know how your partner views you. You will also know what you can do to overcome what your partner considers weaknesses.

Exercise 1: Your Partner's Strengths as You Perceive Them

On separate sheets of paper, list and *describe* what you consider your spouse's major strengths—current ones as well as those that initially attracted you to him or her. Put an asterisk (*) next to any strengths that existed at one time but are *not* now present.

After each of you has completed your list, *take turns* reading all the *nonasterisked* items only. Both of you will enjoy this exercise. After all, we all like to hear nice things about ourselves.

If you have also listed strengths that are no longer present, save them for the next exercise. *Do not read asterisked items now.*

When both of you have finished reading your respective lists, go on to Exercise 2.

Exercise 2: Your Partner's Weaknesses as You Perceive Them

On a separate piece of paper, list and *describe* behaviors and attitudes your spouse exhibits that you perceive as personality or character weaknesses. Be sure to include the asterisked items from the previous exercise, since one-time strengths that no longer exist can be considered weaknesses. Whoever decides to begin must go through the *entire* list, using the following procedures.

1. After reading an item on the list, discuss it fully, observing

the principles regarding giving and receiving criticism presented in Part I of this book. Remember: all criticism is valid from the critic's perspective; criticize the act, not the person.

2. When an item is read and you, as the listener, don't understand or don't see it the same way, *ask* why this quality is perceived as a weakness.
3. As listener, next ask for suggestions that might help you overcome the stated weakness.
4. Only when you have completed your discussion of an item on your list should you go on to the next one.
5. When all items on your list have been read, allow your partner to go through his or her list, employing the same procedures.

The following examples illustrate how this exercise should be approached.

Dialogue 1

SHE: You are not as considerate as you once were.

HE: I'm not? I thought I was.

SHE: Actually, you are most of the time. But, when I occasionally ask for your help, I get the feeling I'm imposing on you. Like when I asked you to make my lunch the other day because you had time and I was rushing to get out, you got mad at me. I don't want to feel guilty when I make a request of you. Now that I'm working, I think we should help each other more. The fact that you don't think so bothers me a lot.

HE: But I made your lunch anyway, didn't I?

SHE: I repeat, I don't want to feel guilty when I ask you to do me a favor. I don't want to feel there are strings attached when you do something for me.

HE: How do you figure there are strings attached?

SHE: When you do things for me grudgingly, that's the way it comes across to me. I feel I'll have to pay for it later. I wish that when I ask you to do something for me you would just do it without making me feel guilty for asking.

Dialogue 2

HE: You're so disorganized. That really bothers me because I waste a lot of time looking for things I need.

SHE: I know I'm disorganized, but I've always been that way. Try as I may, I can't solve that problem.

HE: Well, I see it as a weakness that really gets to me.

SHE: Look, since you're much more organized than I am, why don't you take charge of organizing this house and the things that are important to you? Tell me how to keep things straight and I'll really work at it.

HE: OK. Let's try it that way.

The main objective of Exercise 2 is to reach agreements on how perceived weaknesses can be overcome. If you both realize during the discussion that a particular shortcoming can't be overcome, don't press. Let it be.

COMMUNICATING YOUR FEELINGS OF LOVE

Basically, the marriage ceremony is a couple's public declaration of their love for each other. They are pronounced husband and wife when they agree to honor the commitments of this union. While the words vary, that is the essence of a marriage ceremony. Because most couples are swept up by the emotions that carried them to this solemn moment, they would agree to almost anything. However, I'm not sure they seriously think about the implications of their agreement.

Although you too were awed by this occasion, you quickly realized that the road to a mutually rewarding partnership is not easy. You realized that there are challenges to be met and perils to overcome. To do so you must honor at least two of the promises you implied when you exchanged your marriage vows. The first, as stated before, is to love each other.

The emotional element of love is, for all practical purposes, unique to each individual. You and only you know what you feel when you say, "I love you," to your spouse. You've probably uttered that phrase many times, but what do you feel when you say it? Does your spouse know what you're feeling each time you say, "I love you"? Occasionally it's good for people to put those feelings into words. Chances are that when you buy a carefully chosen card you express your feelings through some professional writer's words, which say what you would like to say but have difficulty expressing.

Now is a good time to make your feelings known through your own words. That is the purpose of Exercise 3.

Exercise 3: What You Feel When You Say "I Love You"

On separate sheets of paper, describe your feelings when you say, "I love you," to your spouse. That is, complete this sentence in as many ways as you can: When I say, "I love you," I feel _____ .

Be candid, honest, and complete in expressing what you feel. Think of the times when you feel romantic and utter this magical phrase; think of times when your spouse has been especially nice to you and the only way you can express your feelings is to say, "I love you"; think of times when you've been apart and thought about how much you love each other. Now, put all those feelings into words.

After completing this exercise, exchange your lists. As you read them to yourselves, you will undoubtedly experience an emotional reaction; it may be verbal or physical. Regardless of your reaction, let it happen and enjoy this moment together. Treasure the feelings; they will get you through difficult times. Also, repeat this exercise as often as you feel you need to.

While the feelings you have expressed to each other are warm and tender, your emotional attraction toward each other can, with little warning, wither or lose its force unless you nourish your emotional love with loving attitudes and actions that bring out the best in both of you. Your love must be *nourished* if it is to be strengthened and if you are to overcome the adversities you may face, together and individually.

These attitudes and actions are the *rational* components of a loving relationship. They sustain and frequently heighten your love, and they enable you to achieve the kind of marriage partnership you originally hoped for. These attitudes and actions are reflected in the second promise implied in your exchange of vows. That promise is to view your spouse as the most important *other* person in your life.

Do you agree that your spouse is the most important *other* person in your life (you being the most important)? If you do, you can demonstrate it by making the most meaningful commitment you can possibly make to your spouse: to get to know your partner as a person and to dedicate yourself to learning about her inner world—her needs and desires, vulnerabilities, values, likes, and dislikes. Only by being aware of what she wants from life and needs from you can you possibly be responsive to her in a truly loving way.

MEETING YOUR PARTNER'S NEEDS

Courtship typically is an exhilarating period in the lives of most couples. Their time together is frequently filled with fun and laughter. They are playful with each other, and their greatest joy is to please each other. In their serious moments, while making specific plans for the future, they talk about their hopes and dreams. Their conversations are charged with unswerving optimism, oblivious of their commitments and the problems that lie ahead.

Understandably, their excitement from having "sold" themselves to each other is too great to think about practical matters. But, as any good professional salesperson knows, making a sale when the customer is receptive is relatively easy. The difficulty and real challenge comes from properly servicing the account, which you must do if you want the customer to be satisfied and not seek new suppliers. Unromantic as it may sound to consider your spouse a marital account that must be serviced, the analogy has practical implications. To be of service to anyone, you must know the inner person, which includes your spouse's current as well as growing needs.

Maintenance Needs

To strengthen the bond that drew the two of you together, you *must* respond to two types of needs. The first type, which I call *maintenance needs,* are *expected* to be fulfilled and, when they are, maintain the relationship on a status quo level and prevent dissatisfaction. While providing for your partner's maintenance needs does not contribute to the growth of your relationship, it does temporarily prevent it from deteriorating. It's like maintaining your house or car. It doesn't elevate the value of these properties, but *failing* to do so can and will reduce their value.

To illustrate the function of maintenance needs, suppose you acknowledge your spouse's birthday with a card or small gift. He would not necessarily be ecstatic, since a birthday acknowledgment is generally expected from one's spouse. Nevertheless, this gesture would prevent him from being disappointed—a predictable reaction if you were to forget the occasion completely.

Some specific activities you may expect from your spouse are bringing home paychecks, pulling his or her weight with household chores, informing you of plans that involve both of you, listening when you are talking, and remembering birthdays, anniversaries, and other special occasions. There are, of course, other maintenance needs, but they vary with each person.

Relationship-Building Needs

Relationship-building needs are different from maintenance needs in that they are *not expected* to be fulfilled. When they are, however, they contribute significantly to the *growth* of your partnership. It is like receiving bonuses. When couples give each other bonuses they feel close to each other.

An ever present threat to marital relationships is boredom and a tendency for partners to take each other for granted. Faced with the routines and pressures of daily living, it is understandable how married people can overlook each other's more *complex* needs. Because they are too wrapped up in themselves, they inadvertently do not think about anyone else, including their loved ones.

This oversight creates problems, since most people are not content with a stagnant existence, having only their maintenance needs satisfied. They need intellectual and emotional stimulation, excitement, and opportunities to develop personally. Typically, married couples look to each other for some of that stimulation. Even if they are capable of coming up with inspiring and creative possibilities for bringing excitement into their lives, they still like having their partners initiate ideas. Why? Because they want to know that their partners are thinking of them.

When you propose doing something special for or with your spouse, you communicate two thoughts: (1) that you are considerate of his desires and (2) that you care enough to extend yourself to him. While maintenance needs can be satisfied in a limited number of ways, only your imagination limits the possibilities for fulfilling your partner's relationship-building needs. Since your spouse does not normally expect bonuses, when she receives them from you you can be sure she'll be overjoyed by your thoughtfulness.

Going back to our earlier analogy, a successful salesperson knows that if he simply gives his accounts exactly what they expect—nothing more, nothing less—he stands to lose them to his competitors. Therefore, he extends himself beyond the call of duty, anticipates his customer's needs, and lets his customers know how important they are to him.

As you can see, fulfilling relationship-building needs—be they words of encouragement, compliments, or actions that say, "You are a very special person in my life"—contributes greatly to your partnership and makes it a dynamic and vital one, rather than a humdrum marriage of convenience.

In the next five exercises you will be asked to give considerable thought to your partner's needs, vulnerabilities, values, likes, and dislikes. This information, which will be discussed in subsequent exercises, will serve as guidelines for responding lovingly to your spouse. These guidelines, which should make you more sensitive to your partner's emotional, physical, and intellectual needs, will also serve as reminders of how you can contribute to her happiness and the growth of your relationship.

Exercise 4A: What Are Your Partner's Maintenance and Relationship-Building Needs?

Separately, list and describe what you believe to be all of your partner's *maintenance needs* that you are willing to fulfill. That is, complete the statement, "I am willing to do the following things, which I believe you expect of me." In compiling your list, think about all of your spouse's complaints and the things he has nagged you about.

Next, on another sheet of paper, list and describe what you believe are all of your partner's *relationship-building needs*. That is, complete the statement, "I believe you would occasionally like it and even be pleasantly surprised if _____." When developing this list, consider all those wishes and dreams your partner has talked about in the past. Think back to all those times your spouse has said:

- "It would be nice if you _____."

- "I sure hope you could _____."
- "Wouldn't it be great if we could _____?"

These are major clues to your spouse's wishes and desires, which are not usually expressed as commands or expectations.

Exercise 4B: What Are Your Partner's Vulnerabilities?

Separately, list and describe what you believe to be your partner's vulnerabilities—your spouse's Achilles' heel. In compiling this list, ask yourself, "What truly upsets my spouse, i.e., how could I and others hurt him emotionally if we wanted to?" While you may have considered some of these when you discussed each other's weaknesses, it is possible that you overlooked some words or actions that could be painful to your spouse. This is the time to list them.

Exercise 4C: What Are Your Partner's Values?

Any ideas, beliefs, or institutions that you prize, cherish, and hold dear are part of your *value system*. It is a fact that two people with similar values are more likely to get along than those whose values are dissimilar. However, they can also get along if they respect each other's values rather than impose their values on each other. In any event, it is important to know what these values are.

Separately, list and describe those *major* ideas, beliefs, and institutions your spouse cherishes or holds dear. That is, complete the sentence, "My spouse *strongly* believes _____." Consider the following important areas: religion, money, sex, education, politics, and family. Those are the areas that are most likely to produce the strongest values.

Exercise 4D: What Are Your Partner's Likes?

What are the things your partner enjoys doing? Separately, list and describe your partner's likes by completing the following sentence: "My spouse would prefer spending her leisure and vacation time _____."

Exercise 4E: What Are Your Partner's Dislikes?

What does your partner dislike or even dread doing? Separately, list and describe all those dislikes by completing the sentence, "The kinds of activities my spouse considers most distasteful are _____."

DISCUSSING YOUR PARTNER'S EXPECTATIONS AND HIDDEN DESIRES

Do you know your spouse as well as you think you do? In this next exercise you will find out how extensive and accurate your knowledge of your spouse is. You will also reach some agreements about what you can and are willing to do to fulfill each other's major expectations.

Consider the potential benefits of this exercise: no more arguments about what you should have done but did not do because you were unaware of what you wanted from each other; no more disagreements about expectations; and fewer guessing games.

Exercise 5A: Discussing Your Partner's Maintenance Needs

Exchange your lists of maintenance needs (4A). Put a plus sign (+) in front of each statement you agree with. Then place a minus sign (-) in front of each statement that you do not agree with because it is not an expectation or because it is stated inaccurately. Next, add any expectations you have that your partner omitted.

You are now ready for your discussions. They will first focus on the minus items on your lists. The person who begins reads the first such item and explains his or her reason for disagreeing. For example, suppose you placed a minus sign in front of a statement that reads, "I am willing to help you with the household chores." You might explain why this is not an expectation by saying, "I don't expect you to help me with *all* the chores. But, when I ask for help, it means I'm desperate. I do, however, expect you to *volunteer* your help when I'm not feeling well. OK?"

Regarding the items you added, read those next and, for each one, ask your spouse if he is willing to fulfill it. If not, discuss his reasons, as well as your reasons for feeling that it's important that he does. The crucial goal in this discussion is to reach a mutual understanding.

Finally, let your spouse know that all of his other statements, those marked with a plus, are accurate expressions of your expectations. Discuss them if you like.

After completing the discussion of the first list, discuss the second one. When you have completed both discussions, each of you should be able to say, in effect, "I know for certain all the things I must and am willing to do to meet my partner's minimum expectations."

Let us now consider your respective lists of relationship-building needs. These represent what your partner believes to be your unstated, private wishes and desires. Fearing that they would be asking too much of their spouses, most people fail to voice these desires. While some may make subtle suggestions, hoping that their partners will respond, more often than not, their hopes do not materialize. It is couples' insensitivity to these hopes and unexpressed desires that creates invisible walls between them and results in stagnant relationships.

In the second part of Exercise 4A each of you listed what you believed to be some of your partner's unexpressed desires, hopes, and wishes. Now it's time to find out how accurate you are and to determine how willing you are to satisfy these relationship-building needs, as well as those that you did not put on your list but which nevertheless exist. Before proceeding with this exercise, be assured that fulfilling these needs will infuse your relationship with a vitality that will bring joy to each of you individually and to your partnership. You will discover new dimensions within yourself and your partner—dimensions that could elevate your relationship to new heights. It will be like having an affair with your own spouse.

Exercise 5B: Discussing Your Partner's Relationship-Building Needs

The procedure for doing this exercise is similar to that of the previous one.

1. Exchange your lists.
2. Place a plus sign (+) in front of each statement that actually expresses a secret wish or desire.
3. Place a minus sign (-) in front of each statement that either is *not* a desire you necessarily want fulfilled or is not completely accurate in the way it is stated.
4. Add any important desires your partner omitted.
5. Honoring the communication guidelines presented earlier, discuss the minus statements first and then those you added.
6. Discuss the plus statements in terms of how your partner can fulfill these desires. Since your spouse already knows what they are, it is now a question of how and when to satisfy them.
7. After completing the discussion of the first list, discuss the second one, following the same procedures.

Two examples of how to conduct such discussions should help you with yours. The first example concerns a man's statement that the wife labeled as a plus. The statement was, "You probably wish we could put time aside during the week to talk."

Dialogue 1

SHE: You're right; I really wish we could set time aside during the week for just the two of us—you know, just to talk about our feelings, concerns, plans, and whatever else is important to us. But for some reason we don't seem to find that time.

HE: I know it's important to you, just as it is to me. But most of the time there are so many other things happening.

SHE: But as long as it's important to both of us, let's *make* the time.

HE: OK, we'll do it. Now that we're both aware of how important it is to both of us, we'll put other things aside and, as you said, make the time.

SHE: Great!

The next discussion concerns the woman's statement, "You probably wish I would initiate sex, rather than wait for you to do it." He gave it a minus because he wanted to modify the statement, since it was not *completely* accurate.

Dialogue 2

HE: It's not that I'd like you to initiate sex *all* the time, but when you're in the mood I wish you'd let me know in a subtle way.

SHE: I guess I'm afraid of being rejected, and that I can't take. Yet I know you would like me to be aggressive sometimes.

HE: Yes, I would.

SHE: But suppose I approach you at the wrong time, when *you're* not in the mood?

HE: I'll tell you what. I'll inform you in *my* own subtle way early in the evening that I'm receptive and then you can take it from there if you're interested. OK?

SHE: Sounds good to me.

One of the outcomes you can expect from this as well as from the previous exercise, is that misunderstandings will be clarified. That benefit in itself makes those exercises worthwhile.

Following the procedures described, discuss your remaining lists, 4B through 4E. Remember, your aim is to reach some understanding about how you can handle, cope with, or respond to your partner's values, likes, and dislikes.

One final reminder: You are not static. Time, maturity, and other factors will make some of your current needs, desires, likes, and dislikes obsolete and will breed new ones. Therefore, it is vital that you make these changes known to your partner. Don't expect your spouse to read your mind. In short, realize that your changes may create problems that need to be resolved constructively.

6

Keeping the Fire Kindled

EXPANDING YOUR HORIZONS

Y OUR marriage does not have to get "old," regardless of how long you are married. Yet many couples tire of their relationships because one or both partners fail to look beneath the surface for new and exciting alternatives to their routinized, humdrum existence. They fail to encourage and help each other develop all those valuable, untapped qualities and abilities. Rather, they bemoan their fate and complain vigorously about the rut they are in. Many detach themselves emotionally from their partners and find new individuals who offer the newness and excitement they can't find in their spouses.

This is not to suggest that you should attempt to remake your partner into your image of the person he ought to be, just as you wouldn't want him to make such an attempt. But you can help each other, and your relationship, by offering suggestions for expanding your mutual and joint interests, skills, and experiences. No one can tell you what these should be. But the opportunities, through adult education programs and other activities, are many. One of the benefits of expanding your individual horizons is that it gives you some new things to share with your partner. That sharing process will provide both of you with a new lease on your relationship.

The following exercise is a practical vehicle for helping each other consider ways in which to expand your horizons.

Exercise 6: Expand Your Horizons

Separately, list and describe two new skills or interests you would like your spouse to *consider* developing. You may, if you like, also list two new experiences you believe would be of value to your spouse. In discussing your lists, be sure to avoid imposing your will or desire on your spouse. You must realize that your partner has a right not to accept your suggestions or requests. With this understanding, employ the following procedures for discussing your lists:

1. After deciding who goes first, begin by reading the first item on your list.
2. Explain your reasons for suggesting the skill or interest you mentioned. Then, determine if your spouse accepts or objects to your suggestion. If she accepts, offer whatever help she needs to get started. If she rejects your suggestion, discuss it further and then come up with an alternative.
3. Continue until you have completed discussing each item you have listed.
4. Follow the same procedure with your partner's list.

The object of Exercise 6 is for both of you to come up with a plan of action for expanding your sphere of interests. You may want to learn a new sport, join an organization, get involved in politics, form a group of your own, or do any number of other things. Whatever you decide, you can be sure that it will enrich your life and contribute to the growth of your marriage.

PUT MORE FUN INTO YOUR MARRIAGE

Loving people laugh and have fun together; they are playful with each other—like children. Doing seemingly foolish but fun things together (either planned or spontaneously) is one of the ways your relationship can stay young in spirit. Suggesting things to do just for the fun of it and following through on these suggestions will add greatly to the vitality of your marriage. While many fun things are spontaneous, knowing what each of you considers fun and foolish is important. Now is a good time to find out.

Find a time when you and your spouse are relaxed and responsive to a casual discussion about how to put fun into your life. The following four questions will serve as a guide for directing your discussion. If you are like most people who have participated in this exercise, you will not only enjoy it but will both be eager to get started on your fun program as well.

Discussion Questions

1. What were some of the things you used to do together that were fun and foolish? Recall those times and talk about them. Cite specific incidents that were especially joyful and crazy. Visualize how you felt when you did them.
2. If these fun times have stopped, why? What prevents you from experiencing some of the fun times you once had?
3. What are some things you could do together that would be fun? Does it necessarily take money to have fun?

4. What can each of you do individually to infuse spontaneity and fun into your relationship?

To help you bring back that fun spirit in your relationship, try thinking of your spouse as a person you are dating and to whom you want to show a good time. This doesn't have to be an all-consuming project. But if you think of it as adding a bit of spice to your life, you'll realize that a little goes a long way.

HINTS FOR HANDLING A NEGLECTED RELATIONSHIP

While you probably love your spouse, can you say you are *in love* with him or her? It is understandable if this question causes you to think about the distinction. The daily pressures of living may cause one or both of you to lose sight of those valuable qualities in your partner that have been, and still may be, compelling. You may become so involved with your own individual small worlds that you could, without wanting to, easily forget about each other.

When that begins to happen and either of you feels your relationship is being neglected, and that "in love" feeling is in jeopardy, give your partner a *gentle* nudge. Let your spouse know what you feel and see that he or she may not. Talk about what you can do together to recapture or strengthen the loving bond that is temporarily weakened.

The importance of making your partner aware of your feelings and perceptions, when you sense that he is neglecting you or the relationship, cannot be overemphasized. Suffering quietly, beating your breast, and brooding about how bad things are for you only intensify your unhappiness. Being a martyr does not win you a badge of honor from your friends, relatives, or anyone else to whom you complain. All these people will give you is pity, which serves no useful purpose. Realize that there is no place for martyrs in a meaningful relationship, since such an attitude creates invisible walls that become taller, thicker, and more visible with time.

By expressing your concerns and desires to your partner, she will know what you want and need from her. Having this knowledge, she can, if she chooses, be responsive to you. When you keep your concerns to yourself, and then resent her for failing to read your mind, you are not being fair to yourself or to your spouse. In the end, both of you lose.

The choices you make in response to feeling neglected are crucial. In the two examples that follow (one for women and the other for men), three choices are made available to you. Which one would you opt for?

Example 1 (for Women)

Monday, your husband promised to take you out to dinner on Friday of that week. It is now Friday morning and he has not said anything about it since he made the promise. What would you do?

   a. Wait until he comes home from work to see if he says anything about going out to dinner.
   b. Prepare dinner, assuming he didn't remember.
   c. Tell him that you are looking forward to going out tonight.

The wait-and-see attitude suggested in response *a* is a setup designed to fulfill the negative prophecy that he probably won't remember. If, before deciding on this response, you had asked yourself, "What would I gain by waiting to see if he says anything about going out?" you would have realized that you were intent on proving to yourself that he really didn't want to go out. Having that proof, you would have felt free to be angry with him and feel sorry for yourself.

Response *b* fails to acknowledge the possibility that he may have been preoccupied with other matters and simply forgot or that he did remember your date but was too hurried to say anything to you that morning. By preparing dinner, which would undoubtedly be done resentfully, you can be a martyr and maintain the feeling that you are a poor, unfortunate, mistreated soul.

Had you prophesied that your husband really cares about you and wants to honor his promise, response *c* is the only one that would make sense. Assuming that your objective is to prove that your husband is considerate, you would do whatever is in your power to achieve that aim.

Example 2 (for Men)

You have been unhappy with the fact that your wife insists on going to sleep before you are ready, claiming that she is tired and cannot stay up past ten o'clock. How would you handle this problem?

a. Brood about it and think to yourself that she is no longer interested in romance.
b. Become angry and find excuses to stay out late, thinking that there is no good reason to be home.
c. Tell her that you have been bothered by this behavior and suggest that you talk about it so you can resolve the problem.

Feelings of resentment and of being cheated will produce the responses suggested in the first two choices. While you can justify such feelings, neither of these actions would result in a constructive solution. Rather, they would engender hostility and lead to destructive arguments. The third alternative, however, assumes that your wife is unaware of how you feel but would want to know. This is clearly the best choice, since it opens the door to honest communication and the resolution of what could become a major problem.

Even before problems arise it would be helpful to agree on a set of signals that will communicate your concerns in a harmless, nonthreatening way. These signals can serve as red flags and suggest to your partner that you need to talk *immediately* because your concerns are urgent. Some verbal signals are:

- "I've got a problem I need to discuss with you."
- "I think it's time for a conference."
- "You seem preoccupied lately."
- "I feel like we're drifting away from each other."

If you like, you can agree on any other signals that would tell each of you that trouble is brewing and that you must make time for a serious discussion.

One caution: When your partner wants to talk, because she is concerned about a problem, be prepared to listen and then take steps to resolve the concern. Do not undermine its importance. Just because *you* don't see the problem, this doesn't mean it is not real. If it is real to your spouse, it deserves your undivided attention.

LIKING YOUR SPOUSE IS IMPORTANT

Of course you need to *like* as well as love each other. But, being human, there may be times when you will not be likable. Some of the things that may make you unlikable include being completely closed to new ideas, being unreasonable, being intolerant of your partner's moods, and being insensitive to his needs. In short, two people can love each other but dislike their actions or attitudes.

When your partner's actions or reactions cause you to dislike her, take time to let her know. Why? Because when you bottle up your feelings and allow them to fester, you again may be erecting insurmountable walls. Since you want your irritations to stay in the proper proportion, you must let your partner know how you feel. Expressing your anger and irritation is essential, but it has to be done constructively. To refresh your memory, here are three ways you can introduce your criticism:

- "It really bothers me when you _____."
- "I don't like it when you _____."
- "I love you, but when you do _____ , it really irritates me."

In the interest of constructive honesty, it would be useful to let each other know what qualities, actions, or reactions your partner exhibits that make him unlikable. That is the purpose of Exercise 7, which is the final exercise.

Before embarking on this exercise, realize that marriage requires you to make certain adjustments. One of the major adjustments each of you must make to achieve a loving and successful marriage partnership is to live with your partner's unchangeable shortcomings and weaknesses. Assuming you love your spouse because his many positive qualities overshadow his weaknesses, does it make sense to focus on the weaknesses?

To help you appreciate the importance of overlooking your partner's few unchangeable flaws, think about the shortcomings and weaknesses that your *partner* has to live with. Would you like your spouse to focus on them? Obviously not. Anyway, wouldn't it be dull if we were all perfect?

If you accept the fact that you can't alter *every* quality your partner dislikes about you, you are ready to embark on Exercise 7.

Exercise 7: Discussion of Your Mutual Dislikes

Separately, list the things your partner does or doesn't do that makes him or her unlikable. Then discuss your individual lists in the same way you have done before.

As part of your discussion, reach some agreement on what each of you can do to minimize these offensive actions. Also reach some agreement on what you can say to each other when either of you violates the agreement.

CONCLUSION

Because of the deep love you share, both of you can affect each other's emotional well-being. A loving word or gesture from you can charge your partner with an enthusiasm for living and a will to excel. Conversely, your rejection, lack of understanding, or biting comment can reduce his effectiveness.

Considering the power you have over each other, you must never abuse it. To do so would undermine the value of your marriage partnership.

Having employed the principles presented in this book, you are now ready to dedicate yourselves to honoring your commitments to each other as loving marriage partners.

7

Renewing Your Marriage Vows

EVEN in the best of marriages couples sometimes forget the promises implied in their marriage vows. They forget why they married and what it means to commit themselves to another person. They also lose sight of the potential benefits that an intimate, loving relationship offers.

On the anniversary of your wedding it would be appropriate to renew your marriage vows. Through such a renewal you can remind yourselves of your original commitments to each other. The essay I have written for this occasion summarizes all the things discussed in this book. I suggest that each of you read it silently. Then make the pledge to each other to honor those vows.

VOWS OF LOVE*

I want you to be my partner because you mean more to me than anyone else. I feel that as a person you have more to offer me than

---

*Adapted from *The Promise of Love*, by Jack H. Grossman (Abbey Press, 1977).

anyone else. *You* are the person with whom I want to continue sharing my life—my joys and sorrows, my successes and failures, and all my other meaningful experiences.

I want *you* to be my partner because I genuinely believe that we could make a better life together than each of us could alone. I feel that by giving the best of myself to you, and by receiving the best of you, we will both help each other grow as human beings. Isn't *that* what a true partnership *really* is—two people complementing each other, feeding on each other's strengths while offsetting one another's weaknesses?

In wanting you to continue being part of my life, I am fully conscious of the responsibilities I am assuming and the promises implied in our marriage relationship. Let me now express my promises to you so they may serve as a reminder of what I must and *want* to do to maintain and strengthen the bond that draws us together.

I promise to love you. When I say, "I love you," I am saying that I care for you deeply, that I feel a special emotional bond toward you and a desire to be near you—a desire no one else can satisfy the way you do.

"I love you" means you are important to me. But your importance is not merely as a physical object with certain prescribed functions and duties. While I would not undermine the value of these factors, you are *most* important to me because of your unique *human* qualities.

"I love you" means you make me feel wanted and needed in a way no one else can. You make me feel that I am a very special person in your eyes. You and *only* you bring out these feelings in me; they are beyond description. All I know is that when I say, "I love you," I feel warm and giving and want to be generous with my time and attention.

But this emotional love that attracts me to you can, with little warning, wither and possibly die unless I do my part to nourish it with loving attitudes and actions that bring out the best in both of us.

Our love *must* be nourished if it is to be strengthened and if we are to overcome the adversities, perils, and challenges we may face together and individually. Because the attitudes I transmit and the actions I direct toward you are vital for building a healthy and loving relationship, let me express what you as my marriage partner rightfully can expect from me—what you deserve from me.

To begin with, you are the most important *other* person in my life. Implied in this declaration is the most meaningful commitment I can make to our relationship: I promise to continue to get to know you as a person and to dedicate myself to continue learning about your inner world—your needs and desires, your vulnerabilities and your values, your likes and dislikes. For only through my continued effort to understand your unique and complex world can I ever hope to respond lovingly to you. Only by being aware of what you want from life and need from me can I possibly be sensitive to your emotional and intellectual pleasures and cater to them in a way no one else can—because I want to make you happy.

Because time and new experiences produce changes in us, you may not always be sensitive to what I want and need from you. I promise to help you understand my changing needs and desires so we do not grow apart. I promise to keep the doors to my personal world open to you so we may build on the foundation that has kept us together.

When you ask, "What is bothering me?" or "Is something wrong?" I will let you know so we may discuss and resolve my concerns. Knowing that unresolved barriers can easily weaken a loving relationship, I will try to recognize these barriers when they first appear so they can be destroyed quickly.

While we face life individually, as well as together, I promise to be with you when your personal problems, those created by the pressures of living, are too burdensome to face alone. My declaration of love means that your problems are mine, because I choose to make them mine—because I love you. When you hurt, I too am in pain. But when you are in good spirits you also enrich my life and ease my burden. Because your disposition has such a profound effect on me, I am vitally concerned about your emotional well-being.

My promise to love you means I would not ask you to give more than you are capable of giving or willing to give. To ask you to be someone other than the person you are would be an insult to you. It is not right to remake you into *my* image of the person you *ought* to be. Rather, my love for you demands that I accept you for what you are while encouraging and helping you to develop those valuable qualities and abilities I know are within you. Knowing that you too want to encourage and help me, I will try to remember that you have *my* best interests in mind when you offer suggestions, directions, and even criticisms.

"I love you" means I think about you even when you are not with me. I think of ways to brighten your day and to make you feel good. I cannot always be imaginative in expressing my love for you. However, I may demonstrate these feelings in little ways—a hug or kiss for no special reason, a gift for no specific occasion, a compliment when you least expect it.

I promise to spontaneously come up with suggestions to do things you would like to do or to extend myself in ways that might bring a smile to your face. I promise to do my part in bringing fun and spontaneity to our relationship. That's how we can keep our relationship young, though we grow older.

I want desperately to maintain my emotional love for you—to continue to be in love with you. I would like your magnetism and glow to retain its force. Yet there are times when I may conceivably lose sight of those qualities in you that are normally so compelling. It certainly would not be deliberate or planned. But the daily pressures of living may cause both of us to become so engrossed in our individual problems that, without realizing it, we could forget about each other.

When that begins to happen, and *I* feel our relationship is being neglected, I will give you a gentle nudge. I will let you know what I see and feel that you may not see. Together we can recapture the loving bond that is present. To preserve our loving partnership, I promise to be as attentive to you as I am to myself.

While I want to like you, as well as love you, there may be times when you will not be likable. When this happens I promise not to keep *my* feelings inside me and, in so doing, build insurmountable walls between us. Because I love you, I must be honest and open with my feelings so they do not grow out of proportion. While these feelings may occur infrequently, I also want them to be short-lived. I will not be afraid to express my anger, but I will try to do it constructively.

Just as you overlook my shortcomings, I promise not to focus on yours, particularly those that are unchangeable. I can do this because all your positive qualities overshadow your weaknesses. Living with each other's weaknesses is one of the adjustments we both must make if we are to continue having a loving and successful partnership.

Finally, I promise never to hurt you willingly. For to do so would undermine the value of our partnership and the deep love I have for you.

I pledge to honor these vows.

Part IV

Questions and Answers

8

Afterthoughts

Y OU now have all the major principles you need to practice to make your marriage work. You also have the tools you need to make your marriage the special relationship *you* want it to be. Finally, here are the responses to certain *general* questions that have been asked of me most frequently during my years as a marriage counselor.

Q: *Is marriage for everyone?*
A: No, just as a business partnership is not for everyone. Marriage, like a business partnership, requires two mature people who are committed to helping each other achieve their mutual and shared objectives and desires. Without that commitment, marriage is no different from two roommates whose relationship is basically marketing oriented. That is, they share certain responsibilities, including financial ones, but for the most part they go their separate ways.

Judging from the high divorce rate, better than half the couples who marry are unwilling to make the commitment this relationship requires of them. Rather, they prefer a marketing-oriented relationship. Yet, they marry, not fully realizing that a marketing philosophy will not work in a marriage partnership.

People whose lifestyles and attitudes are not partner oriented might consider other arrangements with a member of the opposite sex. Why? Because as difficult as it is to maintain a harmonious business partnership, it is even more difficult to establish a healthy marriage. The fact is that an intimate human relationship is far more complex than a business relationship.

Because many couples are becoming aware of this fact, they choose to live with each other rather than marry. If, however, they want to have children, they might consider making the appropriate commitment to each other and learning how to honor it.

Q: *Why are there so many divorces?*
A: Too many people marry for wrong or superficial reasons in the same way that a person might accept a job strictly because of the lure of money. As attractive as financial incentives are initially, they lose their appeal when the job itself proves not to be interesting or challenging and when the person becomes accustomed to the money. Disillusioned that money does not buy him those things he really is searching for in a job, he begins to look for greener pastures. Or he may settle into the job, constantly complaining about his lot in life.

Similarly, couples who are attracted to each other by superficial forces become restless and look to other people and activities to fill the void. When that happens, couples become emotionally divorced from each other, and they may remain distant for some time. Eventually they take legal steps to dissolve their marriage.

Another reason for divorces is that couples outgrow each other. Failing to accept change as a natural evolutionary process in their relationship, they insist on pigeonholing their spouses. When one breaks out of the prescribed mold, while the other spouse either refuses to or insists on maintaining her position about what each role "should" be, communication problems arise. These problems frequently result in bitter arguments, which lead to insurmountable barriers.

Still another reason for divorces is couples' failures to discuss their current and changing needs. Rather, they assume that their partners can't or won't fulfill them. Convinced of the validity of their assumptions, they build a case in their own mind to justify their emotional divorce. Having done that, they seek out others who they believe will be responsive to them.

There are undoubtedly other reasons why couples divorce. For the most part, however, it all boils down to one or both partner's failure to discuss their differences and negotiate a mutually satisfying plan for resolving them.

Q: *Should we stay together for the sake of the children?*
A: Look at it from the child's point of view. How would you feel if you witnessed two people you love dearly hurt each other? Do you take sides or remove yourself emotionally and/or physically from the situation to protect yourself from the hurt that you are feeling? Neither alternative is good for the child. Adults I have known, who grew up in households in which their parents fought all the time, have told me they would have preferred divorce to their parent's staying together "for the sake of the children."

Don't kid yourself. Children sense tension in a household, and frequently they react to it in ways that are damaging to them. Parents who are at each other's throats all the time and would rather not live with each other would do their children a favor by divorcing. In so doing they at least provide the children with two *individual* parents to love and who will love them. This certainly is more tolerable and less painful to children than being around parents whose emotional energies are diverted toward making each other miserable. Being emotionally drained, they are left with very little to give to their children.

Q: *When does romance leave the marriage?*
A: When you let it. Romance is the emotional manifestation of couples' love for each other. People basically do not forget *how* to romance a member of the opposite sex; they just don't think about

doing it. Businesspeople talk about "romancing" their prospective or current clients, which means doing those things that make the client feel needed and important. Some businesspeople take clients out to dinner or lunch, send them gifts, give them tickets to concerts or sporting events, and do any number of other things to maintain a close bond, which they believe will generate more business.

Couples can also romance each other by doing those things that will be emotionally pleasing to their partners. An occasional dinner out, a weekend away, an inexpensive gift, a goodwill gesture—anything that says "you're special" is romance.

Couples who fail to romance each other do not realize that there is more to their relationship than the everyday things they expect from each other. They do not realize that they can bring emotional excitement to their marriage. All it takes is a little imagination!